SEEK THE HEART

Featuring 20 Tales of Triumph Including One by Dr. Temple Grandin

COMPILED BY KARA O'DANIEL

Seek The Heart: Featuring 20 Tales of Triumph Including One By Dr. Temple Grandin

ISBN: 978-1-23456-789-0

Library of Congress Cataloging-in-Publication Data

Seek The Heart /Compiled by Kara O'Daniel
ISBN: 978-1-965971-09-3
Library of Congress Control Number: 2025904175

Visit SeekTheHeart.com for a special gift.

TABLE OF *Contents*

From the Compiler
DEDICATION

This book is dedicated to all the authors who poured their hearts into writing their chapter for this book.

These are ordinary people who have extraordinary stories to tell. Some of them are seasoned writers, others took the plunge to write for the very first time.

As the compiler of *Seek the Heart* I am proud of each and every one of them!

FOREWORD

Dr. Fern Kazlow

"Step up more! You only have so much time! We only get so many chances." One morning I woke up hearing a voice: adamant, clear, urgent. I knew this message was meant not just for me, but also for my friends, family, clients—for everyone in my life and beyond.

"But I do step up," I thought. I was already focused on living from my heart—fully and purposefully. That was at the core of my work. And yet, deep down, I knew there was more to be, more to do, more of a difference I could make.

A few weeks later, I found a lump. I knew right away it was cancer. But my journey with cancer didn't start there. It began when I was a young child. Cancer was a looming, ominous presence in my family. It ran rampant on my mother's side—several aunts I adored battled breast cancer, and one recovered in my home after a radical mastectomy. My grandfather, my world, died of cancer when I was 12. He had promised to be there for my 13th birthday, but it was a promise he couldn't keep. My world was shattered.

My mother's prediction, as early as I can remember, was: "It's not if you'll get cancer, it's when." While it was a horrible burden to lay on your daughter, I understand her fear now. Our family history and a host of high-risk factors made it likely. From the time I was 18, I was told multiple times that I had cancer, or might have cancer. I was told I could've, should've, or might die. While I did get nervous, I never truly believed it. And, clearly, I'm still here.

This time was different; it was real. My reaction surprised me. A quiet, powerful calm came over me. When the doctor confirmed it, I didn't falter. I was resolute. Game on!

I immediately connected this diagnosis to the voice I had heard weeks earlier. "Step up more!" It echoed in my mind, and I knew this was my chance to do just that. A cancer diagnosis forces you to stare death in the face, presenting a crucial choice: to embrace life fully or to retreat. I chose to embrace it, driving me to listen even more deeply to my heart. This experience not only transformed my personal journey but also crystallized a profound truth about the nature of life itself.

This experience became a powerful lens, focusing my view of both my life and the world around me. It brought into sharp relief an insight I'd long recognized: life gives us many chances, but only so many. Each challenge, each setback, each moment of crisis carries within it the seeds of transformation—if we're willing to look beyond the surface and seek its richer message.

My path to this realization was far from straightforward, filled with twists and turns. This wasn't a new concept for me, but one I'd been grappling with throughout a lifetime of health struggles and other gut-wrenching experiences. Years ago, for instance, I found myself on a gurney in the corridor of an Emergency Room after a life-threatening accident. Even as I lay there, wracked with pain and barely conscious from heavy medication, my thoughts were, "How will I use this to grow?" and "How can I use this experience to help my psychotherapy patients?"

I wore this ability to pursue growth in the face of adversity like a badge of honor—a trait I've seen in many high performers I work with. It seemed to propel us forward, yet beneath the surface, it hid a paradox: the relentless drive that powered our success also sowed stress and unseen obstacles. By pushing through no matter what, we sidestepped the vital work of integration, quietly eroding our health, relationships, business—even our joy.

Despite my early thoughts about my resilience and fortitude, it wasn't until years later that I realized a crucial truth: I hadn't truly integrated these experiences into my life. I had missed a key part of the process. This revelation was humbling, but it opened my eyes to a fuller understanding of how life works.

These events that we often view as unfortunate accidents of nature are, in fact, the very fabric of how the universe operates. They are stepping stones, springboards, designed to propel us toward growth and self-discovery. But only if we approach them with an open heart and a willingness to learn.

While navigating immense challenges, I learned a new understanding of the phrase "love conquers all." It doesn't mean everything works out the way we want—our child may still struggle with illness, and we may still face serious disabilities or hurdles. But coming from the heart and choosing love changes us fundamentally, altering how we perceive and work through life's hardships. It turns obstacles into gateways for growth and deeper understanding.

As I faced this life-altering diagnosis, I turned to a three-step process I'd developed to navigate mental, emotional, physical, and spiritual challenges—my own and my patients. This approach embodies the essence of seeking the heart in every situation.

- Be present.
- Open your heart, come from love.
- Be discerning but not judgmental.

This process guided me through the toughest times in my life, teaching me to truly come from the heart in every situation. It hasn't always changed things as much as I'd like, but it has grown me profoundly. It's helped me face life's hardships with more love, more grace, and a willingness to grow. It has helped me accept what is and who others are, even when I've vehemently wished it was different.

My encounter with cancer and other life trials exemplifies how even the most formidable ones can become gateways to exponential personal growth and deeper connection—if we approach them with an open heart. At its essence, *Seek the Heart* is about these gateways—portals to radical creativity, courage, and infinite possibilities. It recognizes our shared, fundamental desire to be valued for who we are, to matter, to love, and to connect deeply. The pain and heartache we experience often stem from disconnection— from our family, friends, community, ourselves, our purpose, and our Spirit. It also arises from our resistance to accept what is, who others are, and even who we are. In today's world, more than ever, we need to come from a place of love, not division.

In this book, you'll find Tales of Triumph, including a powerful chapter by Dr. Temple Grandin and contributions from other remarkable individuals. Each story is a testament to the transformative power of reframing life's most daunting situations as opportunities for growth, of choosing love amid adversity.

As you read these deeply personal accounts, I invite you to look beyond the surface-level narrative of overcoming obstacles. Instead, consider how each author's experience served as a gateway to a greater understanding of themselves and their place in the world, embodying the essence of heart-centered living. Notice how these pivotal moments, often seen as life-altering in the most devastating sense, became catalysts for personal evolution, meaningful connection, and a richer life.

To guide you on this journey, at the end of the forward, you'll find Reflection Questions. They're designed to help you apply the insights from each story to your own life, recognizing and stepping through the gateways that your challenges present, always leading with the heart.

Remember, the path to living your best life emotionally, physically, and spiritually isn't about avoiding life's difficulties or pushing through them as quickly as possible. It's about recognizing these moments as invitations to go deeper, to connect more fully with your inner strength and purpose, and to seek what matters in all circumstances.

Choosing love and connection, we weave a richer life—a tapestry spanning our closest bonds to our humanity. The path to infinite possibilities is yours. Are you ready to reframe hardship and unleash growth, to harness true power and fortitude? Join me, embrace every challenge, and triumph with love.

REFLECTION QUESTIONS

At the end of each chapter:

- How does this story resonate with your own life experiences?
- What insights or lessons can you glean from the author's journey?
- How might applying these lessons transform your approach to life's challenges?

At the end of the book:

- What were your biggest takeaways and "aha" moments from the stories shared in this book? How have these insights shifted your perspective on navigating life's challenges?
- What common themes or universal lessons did you identify across the different tales of triumph? How can you apply this wisdom to your own journey?
- Which specific tools, practices, or approaches from the authors resonated with you most? How can you begin integrating them into your daily life to cultivate greater resilience and heart-centered living?
- In what ways do you feel called to "seek the heart" more intentionally in your relationships, work, and personal growth?

What positive changes do you anticipate as you embody this principle more fully?

- Distill your key learnings into a personal mission statement or mantra for heart-centered living.

- How will you remind yourself of this intention amid life's ups and downs?

Dr. Fern Kazlow
FOUNDER, THE POWER COLLABORATIVE

Dr. Fern Kazlow

Dr. Fern Kazlow believes that whether you shatter limitations – or create them – comes down to mastering your Power Drivers and the field of consciousness from which they emerge. These forces shape your state of mind, define your success, and influence every dimension of your life.

An integrative psychotherapist, speaker, and author, Dr. Kazlow pioneered the Integrative Therapy methodology and established one of the world's first holistic centers. With over 100K hours of experience, she has developed breakthrough approaches to mind-body healing, peak performance, and success.

From this, she created the Kazlow Method: Power Matrix, forging a paradigm that shifts you from limitation to greater creativity, courage, and infinite possibilities.

Dr. Kazlow challenges high-achievers to transform their ideas, passion, and mission into extraordinary outcomes. Where most see obstacles, she sees gateways – portals for growth, power, and unlocking potential.

Frequently cited as #1 authority in Peak Performer Resistance, Dr. Kazlow has a column at Newsmax interviewing business leaders and is writing a book series to help you master the Power Matrix – unlocking potential, developing fortitude, and creating a life of purpose and joy.

HOPE HAPPENS HERE

Courtney Kaplan

Resilience is a word we often hear but its true meaning becomes clear only when we face life's most daunting challenges. Resilience is the ability to adapt and recover from adversity, but more than that, it is the story of hope that blossoms in the most unexpected places. My journey is a testament to this, a journey marked by profound loss, relentless struggle, and the incredible power of hope.

THE DARKEST DAY

It was May, just another hot summer day in sunny Las Vegas, Nevada. My 18-year-old son, Michael, stopped by the house after school and dropped off his graduation cap 'n 'gown, tickets to the graduation ceremony for the following week, and shared a quick greeting. Shortly after returning home, Michael's best friend called and asked for some help with his school work, so off he went.

I was at work seeing my patients when the phone rang. The details of that day are etched in my memory with painful clarity: the phone call that shattered my world, the disbelief, and the suffocating grief that followed. Losing a child is a pain that no words can adequately describe. It is a deep, soul-wrenching agony that leaves you questioning everything you ever believed about life and its fairness.

As a single parent to five children, the weight of this loss was almost unbearable. Michael was not just my son; he was a beacon of light in our family, a young man full of dreams and potential. His absence created a void that seemed impossible to fill. The days that followed his death were a blur of tears, anger, and overwhelming sadness. It felt as if my world had stopped spinning, and I was trapped in a nightmare from which there was no escape.

THE STRUGGLE TO SURVIVE

Amid this unbearable grief, I still had to be a mother to my four other children. I still had the responsibility of maintaining my household. They needed me, perhaps more than ever, and I had to find a way to navigate this sea of sorrow without losing myself completely. Being a single parent had always been challenging, but now it felt like an insurmountable task. The daily struggles of raising five children on my own were amplified by the grief that permeated every aspect of our lives. I experienced my loss as a mother. His siblings were left with a hole and absence that left them in anguish as well. Balancing my grief and attending to their broken souls was excruciating.

Financial stress was a constant companion. As a single parent, I worked long hours in the healthcare field to provide for my family. Balancing work and home life was always a delicate dance, but after Michael's death, it felt like I was walking a tightrope over a bottomless pit. I found solace in serving others. While navigating my own challenges, serving others gave me an outlet, a waymaker for lighter days. Each day had its battle to keep going, to keep putting one foot in front of the other, even when all I wanted to do was curl up and let the world pass me by. Some days were easier than others. That's grief for you.

Emotionally, I was a silent wreck. Grief is a complex and often isolating experience. It manifests in waves, sometimes hitting you with the force of a hurricane, other times creeping up on you like a thief in the night. There were days when I could barely get out of bed, when the weight of my loss seemed too heavy to bear. But in those darkest moments, I found tiny flickers of hope. I call them The Gifts of Grief.

FINDING STRENGTH IN COMMUNITY

One of the first steps towards healing was finding support. Grief can be incredibly isolating, but I soon realized that I was not alone. There were others who had walked this path before me, who had faced similar losses and survived. I reached out to support groups for parents who had lost children, and in these spaces, I found a sense of community and understanding that was profoundly healing. Two weeks after Michael's passing, I began volunteering at Nevada Donor Network. It was here where I found the hope and strength to find one foot in front of the other.

My son Michael's loss came with hope, strength, and a second chance at life. A year prior to my son's motorcycle accident, Michael said 'YES', to organ, tissue, and eye donation. We had a conversation surrounding such a decision, making the family aware of his wishes. After the news of Michael's injuries, our family needed to make the final determination on his fate. Upholding Michael's wishes to be an organ, tissue, and eye donor, hope suddenly reappeared and I began my second chance at life too. Michael saved the lives of 7 people and enhanced the lives of over 75 others through his tissue and ocular donation. These, my dear friend, are the Gifts of Grief.

Sharing my story with others who understood my pain was a powerful experience. So many people continue to suffer from the pangs of grief. Finding light in your greatest darkness can seem an impossible hope. This is when the power of connection and community can make the difference in the lonely world without our loved ones. I have found peace and healing in speaking about my experience, writing pen to page, and outreach efforts, all leading to connection, something we all need. From the seed of hope grows the possibility that one can survive and even thrive after such devastating losses.

THE POWER OF PURPOSE

Out of my deepest pain, a sense of purpose began to emerge. I realized that I wanted to help others who were struggling with grief and loss. This desire to give back, to turn my pain into something meaningful, became a driving force in my life. I began volunteering with local organizations that supported bereaved families and eventually became involved with a pediatric hospice agency.

Working with other families facing the uncertainty and fear that comes with terminal illness and loss was incredibly rewarding. It was a way to honor Michael's memory and to keep his spirit alive. In helping others, I found a renewed sense of purpose and a reason to keep going, even on the hardest days. One such little warrior came into my life and changed me in ways I have yet to fully understand.

I will share a story with you about a brave and courageous li'l man named AJ. I met AJ and his momma at a local hospital in Las Vegas on the oncology floor. AJ's light and smile illuminated hearts and any room he was in. His journey was one filled with many challenges, the first being at seven months old. AJ's little heart was unable to function normally requiring a heart transplant to survive. You can imagine the fear and heartache for his family; hoping for the best yet knowing the risks involved. AJ fully recovered from his transplant surgery and went on to live a full and active life. Bass fishing and video games kept him a very busy li'l man. Being the middle child, he had an older playmate and a younger one. Everyone's favorite friend.

Now eight years old, during a follow-up at his transplant center, labs and tests were run to ensure his li'l ticker was up for the task. It was during this routine check-up the doctors received some very alarming test results. It appears AJ has a rare form of liver cancer, very aggressive. It had traveled throughout his body causing major concerns for his overall prognosis. They immediately began treatment, hoping to slow the progression and buy more time. The news of his diagnosis sent a shock wave that was palpable. From March until June, AJ and his family spent many days and nights in and out of the hospital receiving therapy and treatments. This is one such admission to the hospital. Today, I met this amazing li'l human and his beautiful family.

I would stop by the hospital everyday to see AJ. We would have fun with 'Play-Doh', video games, and puzzles. Sometimes, we would disconnect his feeding pump from the wall, and walk around the hallway greeting onlookers and local fans. He was a true celebrity, loved and cherished. One thing you would always see was AJ's smile. From ear to ear, no matter the pain or discomfort within, his love for life was felt in every smile. Due to the amazing care he received, AJ was able to spend some time at home with his family, making memories, and loving life again.

A week later, it was clear AJ's disease had progressed and he needed the care and guidance of the doctors and nurses at the hospital. I stopped by during my Friday rounds to peek in on li'l man and his family. He was surprisingly alert, drinking juice, and snacking on crackers. 'Paw Patrol' was on loop and so was the family. At any given time, there were at least six family members spending precious time with AJ. All of us, hoping for the best, realistically knowing the uncertainty and grave nature of his health.

Saturday, during my weekend errands with my husband, I received a text from mom, 'Can you please come to the hospital?' My heart sank in my chest and tears began to puddle in my lower eyelid. "Baby", I said, "can you please drop me off at the hospital? It's my li'l man, they need me". Within 15 minutes, I made it up to the floor. I headed to his room. The door was closed. On the outside of the door was a note stating, 'Check with Nurses Station before entering'. Again, my heart sank even deeper. With a gentle knock,

I slowly entered his room. The door swung open and presented a scene like the velvet curtains on opening night on Broadway. This scene was one from life's greatest tragedies. Surrounding AJ's bed were his grandparents, mom and dad, uncles and aunts, and now me. Li'l man was unresponsive, shallow breaths, and pain-free. I couldn't help but reflect on our brief journey together. In the short time we shared, the impact he had on my life, the inspiration and resilience AJ possessed in such a young life is nothing short of extraordinary.

We spent the next couple hours sharing AJ memories, funny stories, and his clinical journey. There were many laughs, some tears, and a lot of hugs. During my visit, I did my best to keep an eye on his respirations and comfort overall. I noticed his breathing was almost non-existent. I made my way over to the hide-a-bed where mom was sitting and visiting. I wanted to place myself as close to AJ's bed as I could when the time came for his release from this world. Mom glanced over at his bed and watched his last breath. She dove off her seat and landed on his bed, scooped him up into her arms and began to plead for his return.

The family ran to her side, supporting her as she was unable to stand or control her body. I noticed the bedside nurse standing on the side of the room monitoring. I grabbed mom in my arms, gently turned her head toward the window and allowed her to grieve in private. Keeping a tight supportive grip around her, we shared an exchange together, just the two of us. For me, watching mom experience pure anguish was both painful and healing. She gave my own grief and loss a physical manifestation. I witnessed what my pain looked like, on the outside. She was grieving my pain with me. I felt it pass through me, onto her heart, and through her fingers as sand fell through the grips of a fist. Unable to control the outcome or the tremendous pain that is now a part of her journey, the rest of her life we share this reality together. In an instant, AJ's pain and discomfort ends and her pain begins. This is grief and unconditional love personified. This is one of my Gifts of Grief.

EMBRACING RESILIENCE

Resilience is not about being strong all the time. It is about finding the strength to get back up after being knocked down, to keep moving forward even when the road is rough and the journey is long. It's about recognizing that we have the power to choose our response to hardship, and that in the choice lies our greatest strength.

For me, resilience meant embracing my grief rather than trying to outrun it. It meant acknowledging the pain of my loss, but also recognizing the love and joy that Michael brought into my life. It meant finding ways to honor his memory and keep his spirit alive in the work that I do.

One of the most important lessons I have learned is that resilience is not a destination, but a journey. It is a process of continual growth and adaptation, of finding new ways to cope with the challenges that life throws our way. It is about building a life that honors our past, while also embracing the possibilities of the future.

THE ROLE OF HOPE

Hope is a powerful force. It is what gives us the strength to keep going when all seems lost. It allows us to see the light even in the darkest of times. Hope is not about denying the reality of our pain, but about believing there are better days ahead. After all, we all have the power to create a brighter future.

In my journey, hope has taken many forms. It has been the comforting words of a friend, the support of my community, the sense of purpose I found in helping others. It has been the small moments of joy and connection that remind me that life, even in the midst of loss, is still beautiful.

Hope is where the heart finds its strength. It is the belief that no matter how difficult our circumstances, we have the power to rise above them, to find meaning and purpose in our struggles. It is the knowledge that while we cannot control what happens to us, we can control how we respond, and in that response lies our greatest power.

MOVING FORWARD

The journey of resilience and hope is ongoing. There are still days when the weight of my loss feels overwhelming, when the grief creeps back in and threatens to pull me under. But I have learned that these moments are part of the process, that healing is not a straight line but a series of ups and downs, of steps forward and steps back.

What keeps me moving forward is the knowledge that I am not alone, that I have the support of my community and the love of my family. It is the sense of purpose I have found in helping others, and the hope that I can make a difference in their lives. It is the belief that Michael's spirit lives on in the work that I do, and that his memory continues to inspire and guide me.

Today, I stand before you a grieving mother, a keynote speaker, best-selling author, podcast host, and resilience coach. It is through my greatest pain, a passion and purpose was revealed. It is my mission to help others find resilience within themselves. Light a path that once was covered in darkness. Sometimes, our greatest missions are in response to our greatest hardships.

CONCLUSION

Hope happens here, in the midst of our struggles and pain. It happens when we choose to face our challenges head-on, to find strength in our response to hardship. It happens when we reach out for support, when we find community and purpose in our darkest moments. It happens when we embrace our resilience and believe in our power to create a brighter future.

Looking back over my life, I am reminded time and time again of the power within the response. While we can't control all the happenings in our lives, one thing we can control is how we respond. How we choose to show up. These times are an opportunity to build resilience and tenacity ensuring we land on our feet every time. These times are extremely important in our development and progression as human beings. Embrace the challenges and revel in the rewards that follow.

My journey has been marked by profound loss and incredible struggle, but it has also been a journey of hope and resilience. It is a testament to the power of the human spirit, to the strength we find in ourselves and each other when we need it most. Hope happens here, in the hearts and minds of those who refuse to give up, who choose to keep moving forward, no matter how difficult the road ahead.

Courtney Kaplan

Courtney Kaplan is a best-selling author, award-winning speaker, and podcast creator and host. With a background in healthcare and a deep passion for resilience, she empowers individuals to overcome adversity and step into their true potential. After the loss of her son, she became a leading voice in organ donation advocacy, sharing stories of hope through her work. As a coach and speaker, Courtney blends inspiration with actionable strategies, guiding others toward transformation, healing, and purpose.

SEEK THE HEART

THE BATTLE CRIES OF NEURODIVERGENCE

Christopher R. Birstler

You might wonder what battle cries have to do with neurodivergence. Let me share a profound truth: being neurodiverse is a mark of strength and uniqueness. It is nothing to be ashamed of. I know this firsthand. Our differences set us apart from cookie-cutter stereotypes—societal norms and expectations, proving that no two humans are truly alike. Merriam-Webster defines a battle cry as:

1. A rallying shout used by fighters before or during battle.
2. A slogan that galvanizes people into action.

For those of us navigating the world with Autism, ADHD, or other neurodivergent traits, battle cries become powerful tools. They can be as subtle as a triple blink or a raised finger, silent signals that speak volumes. Imagine a person who stutters, using a discreet eye signal to request patience from listeners. These are our weapons against a world not built for minds like ours.

You likely already wield battle cries without realizing it. My nightly door-locking ritual, my morning alarm checks, my meticulous schedule reviews—these aren't mere habits. They're declarations of self-reliance, of control over my environment. By elevating these acts to "battle cries," we infuse them with power and purpose.

Consider your own life. What daily actions fortify you against chaos? What gestures or routines center you? These are your battle cries in the making. They don't need to be complex; their power lies in their personal significance.

As I write, I'm forging a new battle cry, a three-fingered signal that says, "I need space." It's a tool I can deploy when panic symptoms overwhelm me or I need to take a breath. This silent signal permits me to step away, whether outside or to a quiet bathroom, where I can engage in guided breathing, mindfulness exercises, or personal affirmations. This moment of retreat allows me to recenter, gathering strength to face the situation anew.

Small sips of ice water will mark my re-entry, a coolness to match my renewed calm. This final act serves as both a soothing technique and a subtle signal of my readiness to re engage. It's a battle cry that empowers me to navigate challenging social waters, a reminder that I have the tools to manage my symptoms even in the most daunting moments.

My journey as a neurodivergent individual has been fraught with trauma and adversity. It's crucial for me to share my life story to provide hope and encouragement for those who are not where they want to be in this life.

Diagnosed at five and uprooted at seven, I faced years of abuse that left both physical and emotional scars. The physical toll was severe: a broken rib, two concussions, a chest injury, numerous sprains and strains, and being physically restrained against my will. Yet, the psychological wounds run even deeper, still healing years later. As a teenager, I lived in constant fear, compelled to parent and supervise the very adults who should have been caring for me. This untenable situation led to Complex Post-Traumatic Stress Disorder at a young age.

Education became another battlefield. In junior high, I faced relentless bullying from peers, both in and out of the classroom. I was isolated, harassed, and disciplined for issues beyond my control. Yet, I found strength in friendships, family, and community support that remain pillars in my life. Even so, I lacked a crucial mentor figure, someone to push and support me in creating the amazing life I envisioned.

High school brought no respite. Students and staff alike viewed me through a fixed mindset, believing I couldn't achieve anything close to my true potential. Teachers controlled everything from my academics, lunch choices, and even my vocational aspirations. One teacher went so far as to lie, telling me not to prepare for the

Practice SAT and denying me access to the prep class. As a result, I failed my PSAT.

But these experiences didn't define me—they fueled me. Today, I excel in college, ace exams, and earn recognition for my skills and experiences. My success is a battle cry against those who doubted me, a testament to the fact that no one defines our potential better than ourselves.

The healthcare system proved equally challenging. As a patient, I was disrespected, my rights violated, and my expertise on my own health dismissed. This led to preventable traumas, including being physically and chemically restrained with four-point restraints and intramuscular sedatives. This dehumanizing experience became another battle cry, a call for self-advocacy and patient rights.

From these ordeals, I learned the vital importance of being prepared. I recommend carrying laminated cards with your health information, emergency contacts, and notes on what helps you feel safe and communicate effectively. Keep your phone's health app updated and accessible to first responders. Doing this will ensure your voice is heard even when you can't speak.

These strategies can be lifesavers in navigating a challenging healthcare system – whether dealing with physical or mental health, or both. In my case, it was my mental health that presented the most formidable challenge.

My mental health journey was a grueling battlefield. Six suicide attempts and five hospital stays across three years and four different hospitals only scratch the surface of my struggles. Yet, each admission forged a stronger version of myself, teaching invaluable lessons:

1. Listen to yourself and seek help beyond what you can manage alone.

2. Recognize your strength and resilience, which often surpasses what you've previously acknowledged.

3. Harness the power of self-advocacy and tap into external support.

4. Trust others when you're at your most vulnerable.

5. Appreciate access to quality care and embrace the power of transformation within you.

I now wear my PTSD as a badge of honor, a battle cry for mental health advocacy, access, and equity. My experiences have become a beacon of hope, showing others that there is light at the end of the tunnel.

Through it all, I've evolved into a #SuperAdvocate, not just for myself but for all who are marginalized. This role was born from the guidance of an advocate who believed in me at my lowest. She didn't do the work for me; she empowered me to fight my own battles. Now, advocacy is the core of who I am, my loudest, proudest battle cry.

I've learned to push through discomfort, to show up even when I'd rather hide. This openness has led to unexpected opportunities —scholarships, mentoring roles, and chances to make a real difference. By embracing my neurodiversity, I've unlocked doors I once thought were permanently closed.

Now, I challenge you:

1. Embrace your current reality.

2. Envision your desired future.

3. Recognize the power within you to bridge that gap.

Your battle cries are uniquely yours. They may be whispered routines or shouted affirmations. What matters is that they empower you to face your challenges and celebrate your strengths.

If I can overcome my trials and align my life with my purpose through my battle cries, so can you. Let your battle cries echo in the face of adversity. In the grand campaign of life, we neurodivergent individuals aren't just survivors—we're conquerors.

Christopher R. Birstler, BCPA

Christopher Birstler is a 6-time suicide attempt and trauma survivor who is on a mission to provide philanthropy, education, and advocacy through his nonprofit organization called From Victim to Victor, which he established to assist victims of crime and service providers from a mental health lens. A Board Certified Patient Advocate, speaker, and published author, Christopher vows to support the vulnerable and marginalized in society until his last breath. His faith serves as a reminder of how blessed he is to be a blessing to others. Obsessed with humanity and education, he deployed the hashtag super advocate to epitomize advocacy as the core of his identity. Christopher is serving on two survivor leader boards and pursuing his bachelor's degree in social work. In his free time, he prioritizes self-care, exploring and meditating in nature, and trying new local eateries around town.

Connect with Christopher via social media. You can search for Christopher Birstler or From Victim to Victor. Invite Christopher Birstler as a speaker for your organization or receive tailored consulting services; email cbirstler@gmail.com with the subject From Victim to Victor Inc. or call/ text my direct line at (718) 883-0004. Christopher looks forward to connecting with you and serving you and others more deeply. **https://fromvictim2victorinc.taplink.ws**

SEEK THE HEART

FINDING MYSELF BEHIND LOCKED DOORS

Kara O'Daniel

I laid there, lifeless. I was awake and my body could move, but I felt completely empty. If I moved at all, my whole world would shatter. The walls in my room were my favorite shade of green—think the pale green of watermelons—with turquoise blue accents. All I could think was "How could I go on?" I felt so sad inside, like my heart was going to shred into a million little pieces. I couldn't understand why.

Nothing tragic had happened recently, my home life was pretty great, but I still felt like my heart was basically in shambles. Sure, I had been dealing with bullies at school, but to me, this was normal. I was in 6th grade and had been dealing with bullies since 2nd grade—I didn't think anything of it. It was my normal. My normal was also undergoing 27 surgeries by that point. This was my life, and I didn't think it was negatively affecting me.

I never really understood depression. I had heard of it, but I was young and never really thought depression was something I might possibly have to deal with. So, here I was, laying in bed in the middle of the day. I was too embarrassed and ashamed to tell anyone that I wanted to die, but I simply could not fathom continuing to live. All I could think was "I would be better off dead. My family would be better off if I were not around. There is no point to living anymore." But I was scared. Scared to die. Scared to live.

Deep down, I knew my family didn't want me dead. My parents and my two siblings are the greatest people in the world. They have never been anything but supportive of me, and never once did they make me feel like they didn't love me or want me around. At the time, however, this didn't make any difference. I was convinced that everyone would be better off if I wasn't around.

I remember it all like it was yesterday. I started crying because I knew if I didn't speak up soon, the intrusive thoughts were going to win. Here I am, in my bedroom, and my twin brother Kyle was down the hall in the living room. He was the one and only person I felt safe going to. "Maybe if I tell him I am suicidal, but not to tell Mom and Dad, he won't." HA! What a joke. OF COURSE he was going to tell Mom and Dad. What did I think? He was just going to sit there twiddling his thumbs while I threatened to off myself? Obviously, he told them as soon as I sent the text "I feel like dying but please don't tell anyone. Not even Mom or Dad."

Mom came back to my room where she found me bawling my eyes out. I just did not have energy to continue. I can't remember my family's reactions. They knew that I had been struggling in school but no one had any idea that things were so bad that I wanted to end my life. I remember coming to an agreement that I was not going to harm myself. I was safe to stay at home until the next day when we could discuss with a doctor what I was feeling, to see what they recommend we do next.

It was several days later that I was able to go to the doctor. I remember seeing a sign on the wall, "Signs of Depression" listing the top 10 signs of depression.

1. Persistent low mood… "check!"

2. Loss of interest or pleasure in doing things you once enjoyed… "check!"

3. Feelings of guilt, hopelessness or helplessness… "check, check and check!"

4. Loss of sex drive… "I'm in 6th grade, how the heck would I know!? HA, I may be suicidal but I still have my sense of humor!"

5. Decreased energy or fatigue… "Meh, I never really have any energy."

6. Difficulty concentrating, remembering things, or making decisions… "I've always been bad at that."

7. Trouble sleeping… "Are you kidding me?! If sleeping was an Olympic sport, I would get a gold medal." The sign managed to leave out chronic oversleeping is also a pretty big indicator of depression.

8. Changes in appetite or weight… "Nah, I'm good. Hmmm maybe I don't have depression after all!"

9. Irritability… "check!"

10. Suicidal thoughts… "That's why I'm here in the first place… check!"

Just by reading this chart, it's pretty safe to say I did, in fact, have depression. The doctor came in to chat with me for a while. She set me up with a therapist to help with my unwanted thoughts and a psychiatrist for antidepressants.

The search for a therapist who I was going to feel safe with was BRUTAL! I've always had trouble trusting women due to the trauma of being bullied by them for years, so opening up to one didn't seem like an easy task. Still, I was desperate, and willing to give it a try. Long story short, I went through seven therapists before finding one that I felt would be a good fit. Some therapists did not even last a session. The first good fit lasted for months before she hit the extent of how she could help. The exhausting search for another therapist continued. I spent the next several years going through different therapists. The ones that fit each helped me in their own way.

Then, one day I found myself in another crisis. This time I was brought to the intake department at the hospital to be evaluated to see if I needed to be admitted for psychiatric treatment. They determined that I did not. However, while being evaluated, I was diagnosed with Borderline Personality Disorder. The National Institute of Mental Illness defines Borderline Personality Disorder as "a mental illness that severely impacts a person's ability to manage their emotions. This loss of emotional control can increase impulsivity, affect how a person feels about themselves, and negatively impact their relationships with others." This made sense to me. I was so relieved to finally have a diagnosis and therefore a treatment that would help me begin to heal and move forward with the life I desired.

The treatment for Borderline is called DBT, or Dialectical Behavioral Therapy. DBT is a type of talk therapy specially used for people who experience emotions very intensely. "Dialectical" means combining opposite ideas. DBT focuses on helping people accept the reality of their lives and their behaviors, as well as helping them learn to change their lives, including their unhelpful behaviors. Thankfully I was able to find a DBT therapist pretty quickly.

I went through the DBT program that consisted of group classes and individual therapy. I really liked my therapist. He helped me realize that things are not always just black and white. There is a lot of gray to consider. Things can be one way while still being another. This seemed impossible for me to grasp. After the year-long class was over, I finally started to understand, and I began to have hope for the first time, knowing that things don't always have to be so cut and dry. Two feelings or thoughts can co-exist at the same time.

Despite how much progress I made with him, after a while I could tell there was nothing more I was going to get out of my sessions with him. If you've gone to therapy, you might have experienced a similar situation where you feel like you've gotten everything out of it that you're going to, and it's time to move on. Well, that time came for me once again. I still wanted to continue on with therapy, just with a different therapist.

I spent the next ten years with a DBT therapist named Christine. Until I started seeing her, I spent my therapy sessions learning the tools and techniques to cope with depression, and the unwanted feelings that come along with it. With her, I began learning to cope with the daily struggle of seeing my self-worth, of starting to restore my self esteem, and continuing to develop my DBT skills. She will forever be one of my favorite people.

Four years into seeing her, I ended up in another mental health crisis. This time the hospital could not be avoided. My grandfather had passed away, and I had just found out I had a miscarriage, all within a very close time frame. My grandpa was my best friend, and I did not handle his passing well. On top of that, finding out I was pregnant, then a short time after finding out I miscarried; it was all just too much to handle. There was also a lot of stress from the secrecy and shame. We were raised that sex was only okay when you're married. The only people that knew about the pregnancy were my brother Kyle and his wife Cassy.

All of this led to suicidal thoughts, which sent me first to the emergency room, and next to the psychiatric ward, a very scary proposition. I had heard stories about how awful it is. Not to mention the movies I had seen that depicted the psych ward as some sort of prison. I imagined it being the worst place on earth. Mean staff treating you like animals, not having any control over any decisions, and being trapped in rooms with people who are out of their minds. Yes, there were some very sick people in the ward with me, but not all patients are as crazy as the movies make them seem.

I spent hours in a locked room in the ER. They have specific rooms for people who feel like they want to harm themselves. Everything was locked up. Every cabinet had a lock on it and there was nothing laying around. Even the toilet was locked away in a drawer. If you had to use it, they unlocked it and opened the drawer for you. It reminded me of the one of those beds that suspend out of the wall in an RV.

After they provided me with paper scrubs, they asked me to remove my clothes and bend over to make sure I wasn't smuggling anything in my privates. At first I didn't understand why they would make me do this, but then after hearing some stories, I understood. For instance, people would hide drugs or other contraband in, well, in the weirdest of places! Eventually I was allowed to put my scrubs on. I was left in the ER overnight until early the next morning when they had a bed in the psychiatric ward open up.

Nothing could have prepared me for what I was about to experience.

Believe it or not—safety, peace, and relief...

I was brought over by hospital security to a locked building on the hospital campus. I was wearing the comfy blue scrubs they provided me in the ER but had none of my other belongings with me. I was allowed to bring certain things but security had to look through it all first to make sure it was all approved items I couldn't harm myself with. Once your belongings were approved, it all went to the nurses station, where you had to ask if you wanted anything.

I was ushered over to a chair where a nurse did my intake. They took vitals, asked me a bunch of questions, told me how being in the psych ward worked, and then showed me to my room. Every room was occupied with two people. When I entered my room there was a girl on the far side of the room sleeping. She slept a lot. She was detoxing off drugs the entire time she was hospitalized, so she was either sleeping or throwing up. Not the greatest thing to experience as a roommate but certainly not the worst.

After I got settled into my room, I joined everyone in the group room. Throughout the day they had therapists leading different group sessions on different topics, like coping skills for living with depression, building self esteem, self-care, etc. They had four groups a day. Usually one was either a music or art group, which were always really fun. Some groups were not going to apply to me which was ok. I was there to take in as much information as I could to help me with my unwanted feelings of suicidality. I told myself "take what you want and leave the rest, but if I want to get better, I know I have to attend all the groups."

We also had a lot of down time where we could read, color, watch TV, etc. I love to color, so I spent a lot of my time doing so. I was a little annoyed though because none of the crayons were sharp. Apparently, this was on purpose so no one could harm themselves or others with the writing utensils. I remember one instance where this big guy was coloring with me, something triggered him and he started attacking me with a crayon. Suddenly I was thankful they were all dull! The staff noticed what was happening and he quickly got a "booty dart" as they called them in the hospital. Basically it's a tranquilizer to help you chill the heck out. I wasn't hurt, I actually found it pretty entertaining. "Wow!" I thought, "If this kind of stuff happens a lot here, I am sure to never be bored!" In truth, it doesn't. There's lots of outbursts from people who want to be discharged because they don't think they belong there, or they want out so they can get high again, but that was about it.

Even with all of that, I still felt completely safe. Safe from being harmed by anyone, especially myself. Outside the hospital there are too many things that I could easily harm myself with. Inside the hospital, there is nothing. There is someone always watching your every move, making sure you're safe and not trying to harm yourself. This provided a deep sense of safety and comfort. On the other hand, being outside the hospital is exhausting. So many temptations to harm myself. Mentally, it started to wear me down.

I met a lot of friendly people while I was there. There was no judgment because everyone was there to deal with their own problems. It felt like a really nice place to meet friends. However, rule number one is to never exchange contact information with anyone you meet while inpatient. We were warned about this many times: never give out our personal information to the other patients. Well, I didn't listen. Now, I am not advocating going against the rules and I am certainly not saying that meeting friends in the psych ward is a good idea, but in my strong desire to have friends that understood me, I exchanged contact information with several people anyway, some of which I still keep in touch with today,

Obviously, dating was an even bigger no no. Well, I met this guy and we hit it off immediately. He was a really nice person and not bad to look at either. We spent most of our days together. We ate lunch together in the cafeteria every day, we sat next to each other during groups, and during our down time we watched TV or colored together. It was nice to have someone to relate to and he didn't seem like he was completely off his rocker. Although he did claim to be the messiah. Major red flag. I definitely should have taken that as a warning sign to stay the heck away. But I didn't. I just ignored it.

Let's remember, I was also a patient in the psych ward so I wasn't completely myself making the wisest of choices. Although I never claimed to be a savior, so I had that going for me! We were both there for suicidal ideations. We understood each other and could empathize with each other and that was comforting. He was a great support at the time.

During my time in the hospital, they messed with my medications in hopes that they could find something that would give me relief. Nothing worked. Finally, they suggested ECT or Electroconvulsive Therapy. The Mayo Clinic defines Electroconvulsive Therapy as "a procedure where small electric currents pass through the brain, intentionally causing a brief seizure. ECT seems to change brain chemistry, and these changes can quickly improve symptoms of certain mental health conditions." I was desperate and willing to try anything, so I was set to have my first ECT treatment the following day.

The next morning came and I was pretty nervous. The only time I had seen ECT being done was in the movies. This was terrifying to me. Back in the day, they did this procedure while patients were awake. I had no idea what I was about to experience, whether I was ready or not, I was about to find out. Thankfully, it was much more humane than the movies make it look. They took me over to the main hospital where I was asked to wait in a waiting room. What seemed like forever passed by when someone eventually came out to get me.

They hooked me up to many monitors, put some electrodes on my head, and that is the last thing I remember. They give you general anesthesia for this procedure. "Whew! I thought. I am so glad I am not going to be awake for this." Nothing, and I mean nothing could have prepared me for how I was going to react and feel after waking up.

Somehow I made it back over to the psych ward and I remember rolling through the door in a wheelchair. I was tired and I wanted to take a nap, but I had completely forgotten where my room was. Did ECT just completely wipe my brain of all my memories? It sure as heck felt that way! I was so scared. I asked the nurse with tears in my eyes where my room was. She reassured me my memory would come back, and what I was experiencing was only temporary, and showed me to my room.

After a nap, I woke up feeling brain dead. What had they done?! Am I going to be a zombie forever now? I had begun to regret allowing this procedure to happen. The next day, I felt somewhat better. I was not 100% back to my normal self, but at least I felt better than the previous day.

The doctor assessed how I was doing explaining in order for it to work, I was going to have to have several treatments. "Yikes, I didn't realize I was going to have to go through this more than once." I thought. The next day, I was scheduled for another treatment. The same thing happened, same feelings, same brain fog, temporary memory loss.

I had a total of three treatments. Unfortunately for me, they didn't work. On my third treatment my heart temporarily stopped. The following morning the doctor suggested a fourth session. Are you kidding me?! No way! My heart stopped. Why would I risk another treatment? That made no sense to me. To this day, I don't trust that doctor and if I ever have to go into the psych ward again, I will make sure I do not end up with that doctor. Now, I didn't tell you this to make you scared of ECT. I know many people who have had life changing results because of their treatment. Many have had complete recovery from depression and are living their best lives because of it. For me though, unfortunately, that was not the case. Even after six-plus years, I still have some cognitive decline because of the treatments.

At the end of the day, looking back now, I had one bad experience in the psych ward out of the many times I have been there. I'll take it! The doctor put me on a new medicine that seemed to be helping, and for that I was extremely grateful. After 14 days, I was discharged.

Walking out of the hospital into daylight and fresh air for the first time in two weeks was a feeling I had trouble putting into words. I felt fragile. Like if I took in too much information or if I said too much, my brain would melt. I reached for my phone, which I wasn't allowed to have the entire time I was in, and turned it on. Admittedly, this was the thing I was most excited for. I was addicted to my phone and not having access to it for two weeks was difficult. I thought, "Man, I am so excited to get on Facebook. I haven't been on in forever! I wonder what I missed?" Information overload! I quickly realized that I was going to have to ease myself back into my normal day to day activities. Something as easy as getting on Facebook, was simply too much for me. Picture for a moment, Bambi when he began to learn to walk. He stumbled again and again. That's how my brain felt but I slowly acclimated back into the busy world we live in.

The guy I met in the hospital and I ended up dating for a little over a year. We had a good time together. We had an apartment together and neither of us worked as a result of being on disability, so we shared a lot of time together. Dating him was a big stepping stone in my life. We loved each other the best we knew how. I say this because I feel like we were incapable of fully understanding how to love someone. He stole money from me many times, took advantage of a lot of things in my life, and I even caught him talking to another girl about how they were going to get together after he found a way to leave the situation he was in. You don't do that to someone you love. I was also incapable of loving him because of my own insecurities, and dating him showed me that I wanted someone different. Even though I didn't think I deserve someone better, I still desired it. As I worked with my therapist, she showed me time and time again why I should not be with him. I worked really hard on building my self esteem and learning to love my life, which eventually meant not being with my boyfriend.

I had a really hard time with the breakup even though the relationship I was in was not healthy. I felt used, unloved, and began to feel suicidal once again. His mom called me one day to check on me. She and I developed a friendship while my now ex-boyfriend and I were dating, growing very close. She knew I was struggling, so one day she called me and suggested I get on a dating app to get over her son. I was very against the idea at first because I knew the particular one she suggested was known as the hookup app, something I was not into. A few days later though, I was bored so

I decided to make a profile. Twelve minutes in, Jon messaged me and my life has been forever changed! We just celebrated our seven year anniversary of being together!

My whole life I have struggled with self esteem and self acceptance stemming from severe bullying all throughout grade school, and dealing with the trauma that comes with overcoming 52 major surgeries to date. This definitely made it difficult to date and form authentic friendships. Until I met Jon, all my relationships felt surface level and a little fake. They were fine, but it wasn't until I met Jon that everything started to fall into place.

Everything about him just felt right. He was a big part in helping me love myself for who I am. Jon is my rock. He has taken care of me after many of my surgeries, he comforts me when I am depressed, but most of all he makes me feel safe. There is not a single person on this planet that makes me feel like he does. He is understanding of my health issues, both physical and mental. He provides for our family, always making sure we all have everything we need. We are best friends and I love sharing life with him. He rescued me from a situation that could have resulted in me taking my own life. I am beyond grateful for the love and friendship Jon gives to me on a daily basis.

Life was great. Finally, I continued to work with the therapist I had for 10 years until I accepted that it was time to bite the bullet and start working on healing the trauma in my life once and for all.

About a year ago, I started with a new therapist. I wanted a therapist who I wouldn't have to drive over an hour to see, and someone to see in person. I was excited to see what this next therapist would help me discover about myself. Every therapist had their purpose in my journey to becoming the best version of myself.

It wasn't until I began seeing Lucas that I realized just how much of myself I lost throughout the years. It was time to work on being my true self. I allowed the trauma I endured to mold me into someone I was not. I conformed to how I thought others wanted me to live, what they wanted me to believe, and I went along with what everyone else wanted, in fear of not being liked. Several months ago in therapy I really began to dig deep, finding out what it meant to be my authentic self. This has been a really fun time in my life learning how to be genuinely happy. Now I'm not afraid to talk about my own beliefs, desires, likes, dislikes, etc. I am not afraid to be me. Two months ago I was terrified to be myself. Now I am learning to live my best life!

I know I've said this before, about living my best life and being happy. While I have said that in the past, and at the time I very much meant it, I know now I was not being real, and I was happy living life the way others wanted me to live it. Living life that way gave me the illusion that I was happy.

But still, something was missing. Until recently.

I have started a therapy called EMDR, which stands for Eye Movement Desensitization Reprocessing. The EMDR Institute defines it as "a psychotherapy that enables people to heal from the symptoms and emotional distress that are the result of disturbing life experiences."

This is the final piece of the puzzle of my healing process. Opening up and being vulnerable about past abuse and different traumas is quite literally the scariest thing to me. I have always been paralyzed with fear that my therapist would judge me, think I am stupid, or think that the trauma I talk about is no big deal and something I should have been able to just get over a long time ago.

Well, I think I can finally say I have found a therapist that I can open up to without thinking I am going to be judged and begin to heal. I am still not perfect. Avoidance is my biggest issue in trying to heal. Lucas can vouch for the fact that I am a master at avoidance, but I know that is actively working against what I am trying to do.

It's painful to relive some of the memories, but in the long run I know it will help me be free of what's been holding me back for as long as I can remember. This time it's different. I am tired of being enslaved by my past, and not living the best life I can be because of it. Working on myself behind the locked doors of the psych ward and learning to come out from the locked doors of my mind and heart has been the hardest most rewarding work I have ever done.

Learning to love yourself, creating an environment with people who you can trust, and working on yourself daily are three things I have learned the hard way that has taught me to become the greatest version of myself. My biggest piece of advice is to get yourself a therapist. I've said this for years. I believe that every human on this planet should invest in a mental health therapist to help process the yuckiness of day to day life and to learn to love yourself for who you are! When you love yourself, you're in the best position possible to love life, and to love others, and love will truly conquer all.

Kara O'Daniel

Kara O'Daniel, a best-selling author and dynamic speaker from Saint Louis, Missouri, is on a mission to be the voice for those who cannot speak for themselves. As a passionate advocate for individuals with mental and physical challenges, Kara's heart for helping others is at the core of everything she does. Beyond her advocacy work, she's also been a client concierge with advanced work in Canva, Google, Microsoft, and more, mastering everything from social media to calendar management.

When she's not navigating the online world, Kara is an avid sports fan who loves cheering on her favorite teams. Whether it's baseball, basketball, college football, or her new favorite—box lacrosse—you can count on Kara to be in the stands (or glued to the TV) rooting for a win.

INSPIRATION FROM THE CHAIR

CONFESSIONS OF A
SELF-HATING CRIPPLE

Destiny Shackleton

Are you touched by life?

Do tears well up in your eyes?

Do you know divine love?

Let me guide you within to meet who you were always meant to be; unrestricted, unrestrained, and untraumatized. We're not infallible; we make mistakes and we are frequently wrong. What if we were all allowed to freely express and develop our talents and gifts? What could this world look like? I want to inspire the light within all of us. No exceptions, we all have a purpose and a Destiny.

You might be asking yourself "why am I reading this?" I asked myself the same sort of question. What do I have to say that hasn't already been said? Who would possibly be interested in reading what I would write? Sound familiar? These self-doubting attitudes held me back for years.

They said you can't be a writer if you don't read. Well, I hated reading, and I did as little as possible. But look at this: here I am, writing; So much for what people say.

I have attended a number of seminars and programs too; I think the word is, GROW myself. All of these events seem amazing at the time but the effects are short lived. The status quo returns within a few short days. So, what is the answer?

For me, it's ongoing. It's making choices, making decisions, everyday. I believe contribution and fulfillment lead to happiness. I believe giving value leads to a sense of accomplishment. I believe we need purpose. Finding my purpose led me here and to write this testimony.

I was born with a rare crippling condition that left me unable to use my arms and legs. I couldn't do anything for myself. I needed 24 hour care. Growing up was difficult. All I could see were the things I couldn't do. My life seemed pointless and hopeless. I was angry, fearful and depressed. I spent a good chunk of my twenties this way. What a waste. But what a gift; it gave me a perspective from which I can share. I was in a very dark place, a place I know many people feel trapped. I can share where I was, what I did, and how things can change for you.

If you are reading this book you probably have an open mind. You probably are not completely happy with the way things are in your life. You likely feel something like: "there must be more to life than this." This feeling of restlessness is a good thing, it keeps us growing and striving and creating.

> *Struggling is an inevitable part of life. Fear can be*
> *all-consuming. Many, including myself, are afraid*
> *of failure, disappointment, and ridicule. We are*
> *trained by society to limit our belief in ourselves*
> *because we cannot completely use our limbs.*
> *Luckily, humans can adapt to their circumstances.*
> *We are resilient and resourceful and smart. If we*
> *can forgive, overcome fears, and put a positive*
> *spin on any circumstance, we are limitless.*
>
> DESTINEY OSTERRITTER

WHAT IS YOUR SENTENCE?

I was born with an extremely uncommon and crippling condition called Arthrogryposis Multiplex Congenita. Doctors told my parents when I was born I would never be able to hold my head up, sit by myself, do anything for myself. My mother cried for three months after I was born.

I really noticed all my limitations when I started public school. I saw what all the other kids could do and I couldn't. I couldn't run, jump, dance, climb trees, play sports, or even do the small things like feed myself or go to the bathroom by myself. I couldn't participate in gym class and I was left out of many school trips. I really didn't complain much but still it was just plain unfair.

As I started high school I was like every other teenage girl. I had crushes on boys, wanted to go on dates, go to dances, and go to prom, all the usual stuff. None of that really happened for me. I was depressed and afraid. I was afraid I'd never get married, never be a mom, and never have anything I wanted in life. I thought I'd never be loved. I hated myself. All my friends had boyfriends and a couple of them were guys I had crushes on. I was so jealous and angry. I was in a lot of emotional pain. I really just wanted to end it all.

When I was born, my mother was sure that one day I would walk. She took me to Germany when I was a baby and for years I received fetal sheep cell therapy in the form of painful cell injections in my rump. I remember being taken to this shaman woman named Cynthia Starmaker. She believed she was a very wise incarnated soul. She had big blonde eighties looking hair, lipstick smeared around her lips, and she played these nativelike drums. I was taken to the front of the room where I was laid on a table and asked to close my eyes. I was told to visualize some stuff and I really don't remember the rest. A few years later I was taken to a church where a healer put his hands on me. I always believed my mother and I thought I might walk one day too. Imagine my disappointment when it never happened.

To clarify, none of what I'm saying is meant to place blame or guilt on anyone, especially my mother. I'm just attempting to paint a picture to explain how I felt. Hopeless, worthless and I wasn't okay with myself. I wasn't enough. I felt like, this just isn't my life; I can't live like this forever. I lived as if I was waiting for my life to start. I wasn't a complete person if I didn't walk and I couldn't really live my life this way. So I was just waiting, waiting for the day that there would be some miracle and I would walk. I became sad, angry and bitter. I was stuck in a win/lose mentality. When my friends succeeded, I was jealous of them. I knew it was wrong to feel jealous but I couldn't help it. They seemed happy and to get all the breaks in life while, it seemed, I had to struggle.

When I was about 24, I was seriously trying to find a boyfriend. I joined all the dating sites I could find. I really didn't have much if any luck. I met almost 90 guys that were all duds. I felt frustrated and hopeless. I went to a three day communication course in Toronto where I learned a lot of very interesting principles and concepts that could help me with my relationships with friends and family. Something else I learned was my "sentence."

This sentence was an "I'm not blank, I'm blank." kind of statement that embodied our true deep down beliefs and fears about ourselves. An example would be: I'm not smart, I'm dumb. We learned that we created this sentence as a child from something that occurred in our environment and our own interpretation of that event and what it meant about us.

For example, in school, when the teacher asked a question and we raised our hand to answer, but we were incorrect, the other students might have laughed at us. We might then create the sentence, "I'm not smart, I'm dumb," and never raise our hand again.

When I finally realized my sentence it hit me like a punch in the gut. I wanted to cry right there. I had always thought that the reason I could never get a boyfriend was because guys were shallow and wouldn't date a girl in a wheelchair. Or maybe it was that I was too fat or too ugly, or just all of the above. After discovering my sentence, I realized I created my own misery with my own beliefs, attitudes and personality. The sentence I had created for myself was "I'm not valuable, I'm a burden." Of course I didn't have a boyfriend. What kind of person would I be to saddle a useless lump like myself on a nice decent guy? I didn't deserve a boyfriend and that is what I truly believed at my core. I was unworthy and undeserving of love.

That sentence was the hardest thing I ever had to overcome. It was at the root of everything. Every fear, thought, limiting belief I had led back to that sentence. "I'm not valuable, I'm a burden." I was afraid of everything, real and imaginary. I was terrified of death, needles, public speaking, ghosts, spiders, being abandoned, being alone, pain. I had anxiety and frequent panic attacks, especially at night when it was dark and I was alone.

AWARENESS IS THE FIRST STEP.

Realizing that the beliefs you have are just that, beliefs, and not necessarily true. This was a challenge for me. Once I discovered my sentence I had some awareness of its power and control. However, I truly believed it. So how was I supposed to change it? It wasn't easy and it took courage and a willingness to keep looking. Keep digging into the depths of the darkness within.

It is actually so much better knowing that it is your own thoughts, feelings, and beliefs that are creating your reality and your life. Realizing this gives you the power because you are the thinker. Your thoughts create your feelings and beliefs. Of course, other people's thoughts, feelings and beliefs can and do contribute to your own. However, you get to choose which ones are supportive to you and which to disregard as inhibiting.

UNDERSTANDING IS SECOND.

Realizing that the darkness isn't you and the endless tape of dark thoughts running through your head is lies. Through understanding these demons that cling to us we can experience compassion and forgiveness for ourselves and others suffering. Now we can adjust our expectations of ourselves and others for less failure and disappointment. Check out my blog for support with this process **https://inspirationfromthechair.home.blog/inspiration-curation/**

So here is what I believe. Every challenge is an opportunity. We can have anything and everything we dream of. The only thing stopping us is ourselves—our own limited beliefs, our own fears, our own attitudes. We create the blocks that keep the good things away.

You may say to me, "Destiny, I'm a victim of my situation. Bad things just keep happening to me. I didn't create the fire that burned down my house. I didn't ask to be raped. My baby wasn't supposed to die before me." I would say you're right. Of course you didn't want any of that. It is perfectly normal for you to have negative feelings about those traumatic events.

What I would say next is this: notice your feelings, perceptions, and attitudes. Allow yourself to have them. These are normal human reactions. This then allows you to respond how you choose. When you have your experience instead of just being it, you then take back your power to choose something different. Everything that happens gives us an opportunity to notice our perceptions and realize it doesn't really mean anything.

CHOICE IS THE THIRD STEP.

Understand that what you already think and believe is true; is actually all made up and recycled bull crap from the past other people's experience that may be completely irrelevant to you. Practice and learn to think for yourself. Awareness, Understanding and Choice; it's that simple, or hard, depending on how you choose to look at it.

The purpose of our mind is for survival and protection, meaning that our mind will do whatever it takes for us to remain in our comfort zone. If abuse is normal for us, we replicate the pattern until there is an awareness of the pattern. If our parents were erratic or abusive, we interpreted the world as unsafe or insecure and those feelings stay with us. Maybe there is the belief that it's impossible to love or be loved. Perhaps they didn't pay attention to us and so we sprout the belief we are unworthy. However, it's all just a made up story, not truth, not fact. Whatever we believe colors the lenses of how we see the world and our very next interaction. If we believe we can't give that speech, lose that weight or live without our cell phones every minute, it's going to be a lot harder, if not impossible, to do so. The same goes for getting through anxiety, depression, or addiction. We start to integrate fundamental beliefs in this world from the time we're in the womb and parents destroy a child's spirit with the unreasonable expectations created by an illusory world.

I hated myself and my life until I was able to look at myself differently and experience a different perspective – a different point of view. This became an ongoing practice to retrain my brain and re-pattern my thinking. I started repeating the Hawaiian ho'oponopono prayer to overwrite my automatic negative thinking. *I'm sorry, please forgive me, I love you, thank you.* Over and over I would repeat this silently. This continuous practice of going inward helped me release old painful emotions and connect to a divine source I had never really been present to. I discovered my intuition and higher knowing that I had never really trusted before.

> *Embarrassment is the cost of entry. If you aren't*
> *willing to look like a foolish beginner, you'll never*
> *become a graceful master. I don't think people realize*
> *how much strength it takes to pull one's self out of*
> *a mentally dark place. So if you've done that today*
> *or any day, I am proud of you. You'll end up really*
> *disappointed if you think people will do for you as*
> *you do for them. Not everyone has the same heart as*
> *you. Worry is a total waste of time. It doesn't change*
> *anything. All it does is steal your joy and keep you very*
> *busy doing nothing. Stop wasting your time worrying*
> *about would've could've and push forward. Who*
> *knows your value is who appreciates you, don't stay*
> *in a place that doesn't suit you". Know your worth.*
> *Don't downgrade your dream just to fit your reality,*
> *upgrade your conviction to match your destiny.*
>
> DENZEL WASHINGTON

Creating drama and discord is what we humans do. We must forgive ourselves and each other to find peace in this life. I'm here to remind you of who you are and what you're here to do. Keep seeking and it will find you. Most people don't find or create work that they love because of conditioned fear. Fear of failure, fear of the unknown, fear of change, fear of rejection, fear of looking foolish and fear of disapproval. It's just a story you make up about what you think might happen or what could be in the future. Fear is the biggest illusion of all but has the biggest hold over us.

What we say matters. Words have power. They are declarations to the universe. What you complain about becomes your focus and your intention, and it expands for you just like it's supposed to. It is the law of attraction at its finest. We are like magnets attracting to us what we think about most.

> *It's imperative to realize that it is not necessary to try to get rid of fear in order to succeed. Rich and successful people have fear, rich and successful people have doubts, rich and successful people have worries. They just don't let these feelings stop them. Your fears are not walls, but hurdles. Courage is not the absence of fear, but the conquering of it.*
>
> DAN MILLMAN

Being uncomfortable is good because it means you are growing and expanding, broadening your horizons, becoming open to new possibilities. If you are insecure, guess what? The rest of the world is too. Do not overestimate others and underestimate yourself.

Limiting beliefs held me back for years. They are usually subconscious and operate below the level of awareness most of the time. You'll typically notice them by their side effects first, often when setting ambitious goals and trying to pursue them. Beliefs are formed through repeated thoughts, and the only reason they hold any weight is because you've decided or agreed that they are true. Try suspending your judgment and take some kind of action to test your assumptions. Seems simple, but these are the basic steps to overcoming any limiting belief.

Journaling is a great way of exposing core beliefs and limiting beliefs. We need to get a sense of radical acceptance of the actual beliefs and feelings that are there. If there is a belief you are unworthy or incapable in some way, you need to call it out, write it down, and expose it. There will be some feeling tied to this belief which needs to be acknowledged and given space. Feelings and emotions need to be allowed to flow freely. Your deepest fears and insecurities will likely be revealed in this process allowing you to potentially discover your purpose.

Observing my own inner growth over the past decade has been quite revealing. When do we truly grow up? Do we ever actually? Or is it an ever-expanding happening throughout time? Do we get stuck, stop growing and die?.. These are the questions keeping me awake at night.. What am I doing here? Why do I matter? I feel like I am still growing, expanding my consciousness, understanding, and awareness. Discovering my destiny is the privilege of my life. Instead of trying to make plans and control, I am practicing just letting life unfold; accepting and allowing what is without criticism or judgment.

When I had given up on finding love it found me. I met the man of my dreams at karaoke not 10 minutes from my house. I didn't need a dating site after all. He's perfectly broken just like me. I have realized that the playing field is actually already equal. Everyone on the planet is disabled in some way or another. Mine is just more obvious and visible than others. I may not be able to walk but my mental gymnastics are astounding. I can reason away anything. I didn't have a great example of love growing up so it was hard to recognize at first but love calls us on to live fully and completely. Two souls intertwine and see that they are one and reflect oneness to the world. True love is astounding and completely worth the wait. Where there is will there is a way. It's never too late. Never give up on love. With love anything becomes possible. I'm always praying now in the background and letting the love of our creator rain down blessings and just let it saturate. Change is inevitable, physical reality is always growing or dying. Divine love is eternal and everlasting and brings peace and clarity to the fretting mind. I'm just here making it up. We all are.

BECOME THE MASTER OF YOUR MINDSET.

Once I started the ho'oponopono prayer and the journaling my life slowly started to change because I started to change. I started weeding the garden of my mind and started laughing and smiling more attracting more and deeper friendships. Cultivating a community of real and lasting relationships that are true and fulfilling is my purpose now. My life is shifting and new and exciting opportunities are always coming along. I am getting speaking engagements where I can share my story of struggle and overcoming fear. Public speaking was one of my biggest fears. I would sweat, stutter and trip over my words forgetting what I wanted to say. After a lot of encouragement I joined toastmasters and just made myself do it. It was a positive environment to practice where I felt safe to make mistakes and grow. I started to see my fear as excitement and that changed everything. Every new day I get another chance to create love and connection with people in my life. I get to choose love and acceptance over resistance and conflict. I see how true power lies in being ok with being powerless. Pain and suffering lead to purpose and our wounds reveal our why. I don't have to go looking anymore; they will find me. Those that seek love, light, peace and truth. I have hid in fearful ignorance but will shine forth as a beacon of strength cloaked in crippling weakness.

We experience trauma and abuse and to protect ourselves hide our hearts. By seeking mine and opening it wide my life is forever changed. The future looks bright and exciting. I hope the same for all who read this book. Namaste

Destiny Shackleton

Born with a unique disposition in life Destiny Shackleton grew up in the small city of Brantford Ontario Canada with the love and laughter of family and friends.

It is this disposition that has driven her to a life that is a true journey. From seeking a cure to finding advantages from a place of disadvantage, to simply level the playing field and create purpose in her life.

There is no doubt in the minds of those who know her she has the right to aim for the sky. And what gives her that right is her continual quest to overcome her fears, and her limitations.

With passion, love, courage and song, Destiny proves that having a disability is no disability at all once you learn the right words. With special interests in public speaking, mediation, and social networking, Destiny shares her inspirational story with the world.

The condition which Destiny defies is Arthrogryposis Multiplex Congenita. This condition develops before birth and involves limited mobility of multiple joints and is comparable to a quadriplegic. She is unable to do most everyday things for herself we take for granted.

HOPE INFUSED CHAOS

K. Crystal Griffith

"Get out, the car is going to explode!"

What was happening?

I had just dropped off my new husband of only 4 months to his first all-day recreation trip he was leading. I remember coming up to the top of the hill, seeing the green light at the bottom, and proceeding through.

Now I was in the middle of the intersection, with a car smashed into my front fender, the driver's door unable to open, and smoke quickly rising from under my hood.

My chest was killing me from the airbags, my arms looked like someone had lashed a whip around them, and I was not too steady on my feet when I finally was pulled from the car.

Life took a dramatic turn when a young girl, who didn't defrost her windshield, T-boned my car. Although I walked away from the accident, I woke up two days later with headaches that plagued me. This was just the beginning of a journey that would challenge me, my marriage, and my life mentally, physically, emotionally, and spiritually.

We had just moved to a new college town for my husband's work with no established friends or nearby family. The constant pain was excruciating. Sometimes, I would wake up not knowing where I was or remembering my own name. Even the hum of the refrigerator was too loud.

To survive the headache pain, days were spent sleeping and avoiding light, noise, and thoughts. If I had to drive to a doctor's appointment, many were 30-45 minutes away from our rural town. I would arrive much earlier than the appointment time to nap in the car just to recover from the drive and brain focus needed to get there. This was pre-GPS, pre-cell days. Having to map out the drive took so much effort and brain power that it would push me into deep brain and body fatigue. If I didn't write things down and put them in the same place daily, I would have no idea what was happening that day.

If it's not on the calendar, it is not in my brain. When we were moving with our first military assignment, somehow my calendar had been packed in a box. We had to empty a third of the moving truck looking for it. No one could understand why it was such a big deal. But no calendar meant we weren't going anywhere. I was visibly relieved when we found it. I was quite happy when calendars went digital, so I'd never lose it again!

My recovery experience with the medical system was quite frustrating as well. A subdural hematoma, a Traumatic Brain Injury or TBI, was found on an MRI two weeks after the accident, but there were no adequate treatments for such injuries, especially for women back then. Additionally, internal bleeding led to an inpatient stay, the loss of my appendix, and losing my health insurance while I was inpatient resulting in a $43,000 bill. Coping with my health was not new for me. I had an assortment of casts all through my growing-up years. But managing this type of pain, medical chaos, and insurance ridiculousness, was all new and I was truly left alone to handle it all. My husband didn't know how to handle any of this and would escape to work or school.

As the headaches increased, I sought doctors for help. All were male and too many would pat my leg, telling me to go home and sleep off my headache. Decades ago the doctors knew very little about head traumas, even with the MRI showing the active brain bleeds. There was quite a bit of medical gaslighting as well, me being a woman with my pain was so high on the scale, they would determine I couldn't possibly mean what I said. Then there was the moment I was admitted to the ER for such a high pain level.

A friend came to keep my husband company. They were trying to distract me from the pain and telling jokes. I would smile. The nurses saw me smile and immediately charted I must be faking the pain and sent me home. Through all this, I learned the importance of self-advocacy.

Not finding any help medically led me to learn how to research new techniques through magazines and newsletters; no real internet searching back then. As I honed those skills, I had no idea how useful they would be through the decades for me, others, and later my own child. Emotionally, I felt let down and dismissed by the medical community, and even today find myself distrustful of their options and solutions for my daughter. I question why they've missed major diagnoses, combinations of symptoms pointing to other diagnoses, and why I have to advocate so strongly on her behalf when it should be their job. It's made me even question what doctors are taught in medical school.

God and I had many conversations along the way of why it happened at all, why my husband hit the snooze too many times that morning, why the young girl didn't take just two minutes to defrost her windshield, why the medical community did not believe me even with scientific proof, why my brain was affected the way it was, and mostly why He didn't just heal me. The last question was the most persistent: why didn't He just heal me? I had no doubt He could. I searched the scriptures high and low for answers.

Those days were fraught with how to survive physically, emotionally, and financially. Nothing seemed stable, and I was struggling with figuring out who I was now compared to before the accident. In the middle of this struggle, I had to lay down my acceptance to a prestigious PhD program. My future dreams seemed to disappear. Who was I to become?

In the middle of this crisis, my marriage became distrustful due to my husband's episodes towards me. When we finally parted ways, 24 years later, I asked him when he stopped trusting me. He responded after the accident because my personality changed. I wasn't the fun-loving gal he had married. There are so many things wrong with that answer but I can't change his thoughts or manage his expectations. While I was having to connect with my new normal, I was alone in doing so. I was now trapped in a marriage that caused fear, trepidation, and more questions about the future than it answered.

In those moments of loneliness, pain, hurt, disappointment and fear, I survived. But the reality set in that I wasn't well emotionally. I had to push through to find the other side. I think this is when I learned to compartmentalize my emotions, or they were affected by the brain injury, perhaps both. The chronic pain and isolation took their toll. Compartmentalizing was not a healthy strategy but helped me survive even while keeping me from fully acknowledging my struggles.

Over time I've had several heart-healing sessions to process that unconscious decision to move through scenarios with little emotion. At one point, it had even been years since I cried. I look back now and wonder if that's because crying caused so much pain in my head physically or that I couldn't handle one more emotion on my own back then. Today, I do cry but it's still rare, even through a divorce, my child having a medical history like no other, losing a business I loved, a few tears, and more focused on what I need to do now to move through it. Moving every four years growing up, making new friends and then leaving them has taught me "eyes forward," to move ahead versus dwelling on what could've been. I've learned to press through life's challenges with resilience, seeing every day as an adventure. The definition of an adventure is engaging in hazardous and exciting activity, especially the exploration of unknown territory. There is nothing exciting about a car accident or chronic pain, but engaging in an unknown territory was and continues to be the unwritten mantra of my entire life. Thus it's filled with adventure.

The accident shifted my world as I went from being an extremely outgoing leader, on track for a full-time career to an introverted hermit, avoiding everything and everyone, desperate to get out of pain. It took several years to pull myself out of my shell to seek others. Today, I've come to a place where I am an extrovert to others but need to recoup to re-regulate my brain and nervous system.

Community support was difficult in those days. There was, and in many ways still is, a lack of financial resources to support those who cannot work due to disabilities. I had lost my well-paying position, my husband was working part-time, and even that stopped when he joined the military. We were not paid for over 12 weeks during his initial military training. I still had to pay bills. A friend ran a shop and offered me a few hours as I was able to come in. I began to knock on every community agency door possible. By the grace of God, I was able to scrape together enough for another month of rent.

I drew on sources of strength deep within me as my husband left for potentially a year and half for the Air Force Pararescue school. I was relieved when he decided that career path was not for him and we reconnected after only four months. During those months, I was living at doctor's appointments, sleeping, and trying to hold on. We had both agreed to the military, which would lead to this separation, but the reality of walking it out on my own was quite more than I expected. But as my good friend says, just another day in Crystal's world.

Walking through dark moments, tough times, and unforeseen circumstances can reshape your personality or build upon it. Learning to press in for answers builds your mental stability and mindset. Seeking hope brings a light that dispels the darkness, even if for a moment. Sometimes a moment is all you need.

I stumbled upon one doctor who did take more than a minute with me, and suggested I try a specific medication. The effects were almost immediate after the first pill. I had two weeks of being back to normal—no pain, no noise or light issues, no hum of the refrigerator driving me crazy. I was back to being Crystal before the accident. That medication was a miracle in itself until day 15 when I woke with a headache. My body had either become accustomed to it or rejected it. It didn't matter the dosage; it no longer worked. Despite the outcome, I saw I could be back to normal again. It was the light and moment I needed. I had hope again.

During my husband's military training, I relied on my faith and the support of our local church. The church couples listened, invited me to events, and showed up in the ER. Their support was a beacon of light during a very dark time. When I returned for the court case four years later, reconnecting with these friends reminded me of the angels God placed in my life along the way.

It was also during this military separation time that my family and I realized I wasn't able to stay by myself, so they came and helped me pack up the truck taking me back to their home. For a family who never had headaches, this was hard on them to watch as well. I was not the same daughter or sister returning to them as when I left.

Spiritually, my faith was my anchor. A friend's mother once pointed out that I had the gift of faith, a lifelong walk with God that had always been a part of me. This faith sustained me through the darkest moments. My family typically would call me out as a religious fanatic as a young child for wanting to talk too much about God. How do you talk too much about God? I had always known Him. I never had a huge conversion experience. At 13, I wanted one of those experiences my friends were having, even though I already knew Him. So I went up to the altar during a church camp. My desire to know Him even more increased after that moment. Thank goodness today, my entire family has come to know Him in a personal and intimate way. So my gift of faith has always been there and without it, I truly would have succumbed to some of the dark thoughts I had along the way. I leaned into my faith, seeking God first and trusting Him with an uncertain future. Despite all of this chaos, I felt firm in my faith that my journey would eventually become a testimony. I don't think I realized the magnitude of that expectation or what God was preparing me for with my child and her many medical complexities.

There were many times I could not handle the day, the moments, or what the future seemed to look like. The chronic pain took over every thought and that's when the dark thoughts would come. But in the middle of those moments, I knew God was bigger. I was already a living miracle for my parents, my time was not up, and my purpose was incomplete. Due to the pain, reading or music were quite difficult to use. Walking outside was hard due to the sun, so I took many evening and night walks when the cooler air would help. During those moments, God and I would have conversations that often sounded like me complaining, crying out, whining, but resolved to walk the journey for the unknown purpose in the moment. Perspective is an attitude within the adventure that shifts it to knowing it's really about what will come from the adventure, living it as it unfolds, and applying all the lessons learned up to this point in life.

When my husband and I reconnected after his training, we moved to his first base assignment. The emotional compartmentalization I had to create served me well at times but also kept me from acknowledging how difficult walking this journey alone was. People who don't have headaches are fortunate not to know the debilitating effects they cause. When we made it to the base, I started the experimental neurofeedback cycles 90 minutes from our home. I drove alone there and back three times a week, for six weeks, while he was at work. I do wish I could say the neurofeedback healed my head but this was new and in its infancy. I did not achieve the results we wanted to see. Those long car rides became a set time to chat with the Lord, hum to praise and worship, and listen. Many never have that opportunity; I was fortunate. The lessons we learn in the hard times are unexpected, never sought after, and bring a different source of strength that wells up within you.

The church we joined after moving to the base was on fire for the Lord, and it helped me find people who could handle it if I stayed home instead or needed to walk away for a bit. They accepted me as I was in that season. During this time, I started to learn American Sign Language at the church as well, and for some reason, my broken brain excelled at it. My brain still working that well was a mustard seed miracle.

As time progressed, I learned some of my new normal limitations. Even today, there are a few residual effects of my TBI that I have to deal with daily. For example, I often tell people the shortest distance is A to B to C but my brain isn't able to find point B at times. Instead, it will create a completely new path A-P-Q-D-C to finally get to the end result. This tends to frustrate me because I know I can do it but my response time or simplistic task can become complicated.

It also can take a moment or two to find the word I need for a sentence. This tends to become worse with exhaustion or stress. I have to say to the person, hold that thought, it's coming, and wait for my brain to catch up. Or I'll find another similar word. I remember one time I could not think of the word ice to save my life; instead, I said water in hard form. We all laughed!

When I taught college, I would share two key pieces in our first class together, whether they were online or in person. 1) There is no shame in asking for help. I had a Traumatic Brain Injury and I had to learn to ask for help. If you need accommodations, ask for them. They are tools to help you succeed, just as a wheelchair or cane assist as aids. Tools do not make you less; rather, they show you are smart in leveraging what is available for your for success. 2) Due to the brain injury, I may stop mid-sentence and we will play a little guess the word Crystal needs to say next because it has completely left my head. Many students would come up to me after that class and thank me for being open and vulnerable, as well as being a role model for showing up well and moving through life despite the hardships. I taught college, staff, admin, and other grades for over 30 years. No gold watch but I cherish the moments with my students of all ages, especially when I can see the learning lightbulb pop on, seeing them achieve what they didn't think they could do.

As I know my students and clients can, You can overcome! You can be all God has called you to be. Your purpose may not look like what you expect, but it is part of what He has seen your whole life.

Despite my headaches and setbacks, I taught at several schools at the college level and for corporations. For some reason, my technology skills never left me, thank goodness. I created databases for the government, franchises, and colleges. I also earned my Master's. I look back and see what was lost was leveraged for what could be, what I never would've learned or seen if the losses had not happened.

As I continue to work on healing, I learn something new about holistic methods daily, whether it's an oil, a device, a new technology, or an age-old remedy. We have so much to learn from those we have tried to discard through the ages by culture, ethnicity, or even age. My uncle, who was a daisy farmer for decades, had a thumb greener than anyone's. His family used holistic remedies, ate from the land, worked the land, and stayed connected to themselves. We all called him our crunchy uncle. Today, I laugh at how many of the same tools I use in my health journey. Treating our bodies well includes being informed of all options, not just the ones the doctors suggest. Learning we can say no to doctors' suggestions, and they are suggestions, not mandates, is empowering.

The advocacy, holistic tools, and connector mentality have allowed me and my daughter to be instrumental in helping others with diagnoses. Just last week another person was seeking out a doctor for a possible Ehlers-Danlos Syndrome diagnosis. We are in double digits for how many have now been diagnosed with Celiac. I've lost count of how many have now been officially diagnosed on the Autism Spectrum, young and old alike. The case management skills I've had to learn have also been put to use in various entrepreneur adventures, supported others, and afforded me better conversations with nurse managers through multiple medical systems.

To share the discoveries, resources, and tools, I founded Medical Mom Warriors™. The more we can connect people with the tools, the sooner they will feel better. When Medical Mom Warriors™ was created, it was a summit of other medical moms, who had special needs children, sharing their stories and education. Today, it has a global reach, connecting with moms in hospitals, doctors' offices, physical therapy, occupational therapy, speech therapy, and some even in airports.

With the resources I had discovered, it was still a daily struggle. Four years into this chronic pain journey, we were at church; the worship was flowing, and you could feel the presence of the Lord. The choir director took to the microphone and began to call out healing for specific ailments. I had been in this situation before, crying out to the Lord to heal my head, but until this point, nothing had been healed. I wasn't thinking about myself that night. A few minutes into this move for healing, he called out "someone who had a car accident a few years ago and has suffered horribly from debilitating pain in their head". I didn't really hear what he said but multiple people I was sitting with began to poke me, saying, "That's you." I listened as he repeated himself. Then the internal war began.

The next morning, I was due to drive back to the original location of the accident for the court case. If I was healed now, how could I share with the court what I had been experiencing, the effects on my marriage, and being told I'd never have children without risking a stroke and death? I felt I would be lying to the court somehow if I was healed. God in all His patience asked me, "Who do you trust, Me or the court to provide what you need?"

"You, Lord."

"Then it's time to be healed."

This was truly one of the biggest leaps of faith for me. I walked forward, and instantly my headache subsided. I was healed of the superimposed migraines I had been experiencing. My friends could see the visible shift in my face and body. This was one of many mustard seeds of faith miracles I began to experience through this journey. Those superimposed migraines, one on top of the other, have never returned. Today I rarely have a headache, usually only due to bad weather or lack of food.

There is a time and place for what I call Western Medicine, but there should also be a connection to holistic options that are non-invasive if they can support and heal the issue. For example, castor oil. Who knew this was a miracle oil? Today, we are learning more every day about what it can heal from the outside-in just by using it in the belly button, across a lump or bump, over the eyes, and more. Note that I am not a medical professional, so this is educational information only. I have been using it in several places with healing results. My daughter is even using it now for many of her symptoms.

Today, because I have so many tools to utilize, my recoveries from surgeries, Covid, and more have been much faster and holistic. I still have to walk through them but I've been surprised how quickly they pass now. The most important tool is community. Knowing no one is alone as they journey through medical issues for themselves or their loved ones removes the weight of loneliness and, honestly, the feeling that you are crazy at times when you have been gaslighted by the medical community.

Surprisingly, God sends me clients who have been in abusive marriages, had a medical condition arise unexpectedly, or have a special needs child. Those He knows need to be heard, seen, and validated. We connect in the moments of their loss with deep feelings because we've both been there. They can also see hope for what can be through our story sharing and seeing what God has done in and through me.

The most important lesson I learned in this journey is to trust your gut. The "should haves" outweighed what I actually did. I should've fought for more medical advocacy, even when it wasn't a real department back then. I should've stopped rationalizing other's behaviors towards me and stood up for my real worth and safety. I should've...

The reality of looking back in hindsight is a 20/20 perspective, but when you're in the middle of chronic pain, a mess of a marriage, fighting for your sanity and life on several fronts, you are doing the best you can in the moment. I had to stop comparing what I should've or could've done because that implies those choices include all of the wisdom and knowledge I've gained since then.

That is not fair to who I was as a person versus who I am today. Ultimately, I found that my life was an adventure. Hope has girded me up in many ways. Walking out strategies of Healing, Opportunities, Perseverance, and Endurance have supported my daughter, friends, and those in Medical Mom Warriors™ across the globe. Through these experiences, I've realized the power of H-O-P-E:

- Healing: Focus on healing inside and out, physically and emotionally. Without taking the time to heal, we cannot truly help others.

- Opportunities: Embrace opportunities to bring in new tools, connect with like-minded people, and innovate solutions for the challenges.

- Perseverance: Show up every day, in every moment, despite the difficulties and stress. Perseverance is an active decision to keep moving forward.

- Endurance: Handle the hard moments with the knowledge that strength is gained through endurance while being fearlessly authentic in the journey.

REFLECTION AND CRITICAL THINKING

1. Reflect on a personal experience that challenged you mentally, physically, emotionally, or spiritually. How did you approach this challenge, and what did you learn from it?

2. What strategies do you use to maintain your mental well-being during difficult times?

3. How do you take care of your physical health, and why is it important in your overall well-being?

4. Think about a time when your emotions were difficult to manage. How did you navigate through them, and what helped you regain balance?

5. In what ways do your spiritual beliefs or faith influence your daily life and decision-making?

6. How can you turn your challenges into adventures and opportunities for growth and learning?

By reflecting on these questions, I know you can find your own path to living your best life, mentally, physically, emotionally and spiritually. Bring your tea and visit with me at **https://linktr.ee/ kcrystalgriffith.com**.

K. Crystal Griffith

K. Crystal Griffith is a Jesus-loving, sweet tea-drinking, renaissance woman empowering Medical Mom Warriors™ with health, healing, and hope advocating for them and their medically complex kiddos to thrive.

Crystal walks with clients through deployments, life-threatening allergies, autoimmune diseases, cancer, traumatic brain injuries, concussions, marriage difficulties, abuse, PTSD, reactive attachment disorders, generational traumas, neurodiversity, and all the things that go bump in the night. These and many more have influenced Crystal's life directly as well. She is a Certified Heart Healing Practitioner, Business Coach, and Medical Advocate supporting medical mommas to advance their reach through their personal experiences.

Crystal, her beautifully creative, humorous, horse-loving daughter, and her service dog Otter, recently flew the coop from the Rockies to the Virginia Coastline. With them, there's always an adventure waiting just around the bend. For a free gift, bring your tea and visit with me at **https://linktr.ee/kcrystalgriffith. com**

NAVIGATING, SURVIVING, AND OCCASIONALLY THRIVING

Haley Gray

I'm not going to lie. The last 8.5 years in my life have been challenging on a good day. It's taught me a ton. Not always in a good way, either.

Every day starts with questions.

Am I going to have to deal with an irate client?

A kid in the hospital today?

How am I going to make it through today? Why am I even here?

On December 6, 2015, my oldest daughter fell off of a horse, hitting her head hard on the dirt below. In retrospect, it was probably right in the middle of her first psychotic break. Double doozie, a traumatic brain injury, and a psychotic break at the same time. Not that we knew what we were dealing with, of course.

She was hospitalized for the first time then and, boy oh boy, has it been a roller coaster ever since.

Consider that our (the United States, at least) entire mental health system is badly broken. Our insurance system is badly broken. If you have a loved one with severe mental illness, they are lucky if they don't end up homeless or in prison.

As some back history, if someone is a threat to themselves or others, they can be hospitalized and held for mental health reasons. But if the person is over the age of 18, some places as young as 14, the facilities can make it so you as the parents have no idea what is going on with care, even if the patient isn't in a state of being able to make good decisions due to mental incapacity.

Plus the insurance companies get in on the action and get to decide just how long someone can remain hospitalized. Imagine, if you will, that the patient goes into the hospital, decides that you as the caregiver parent can't talk to the doctor, or insurance (even if the parent is paying the bills!), and then we go in circles.

The patient can be completely homicidal, with a plan to kill someone, and the insurance can be like "Oh, they can be discharged now." In fact, there were multiple times when my oldest was discharged from the hospital while actively homicidal and journaling about it. She texted her friend that she was thinking about killing the entire family but hadn't acted on the impulse because she hadn't figured out what to do with our bodies. Um. Great. Sounds like she should TOTALLY be discharged.

Needless to say, when we got the screenshot of those texts, we called 911, and had her hospitalized. They kept her for just over 3 weeks, discharging her to a "step down" or partial hospitalization program.

The partial hospitalization program discharged her after three days because she was "too psychotic" and was upsetting the other patients. She made it less than three more days before the next hospitalization.

After almost 19 hospitalizations, going back and forth, I was able to obtain legal guardianship. That meant 19 suicide attempts and multiple homicidal attempts while going back and forth with medical providers and insurance companies.

In fact, in a stretch in 2019, she was in and out of the hospital almost constantly, despite having self-admitted homicidal ideations. She'd go in, be there a few weeks, have her meds changed and still be homicidal; but her time was up, so they would discharge her. The longest she was at home was three weeks. Our current, shortest record between hospitalizations was set in 2023, with less than 9 hours out of the hospital.

In the background, I was trying to grow a business, manage employees and contractors, and stay semi-sane. Mind you, there is absolutely NOTHING sane in growing a business.

By October 2018, my weight had ballooned to 427 pounds. It became clear that in the world of trying to manage my daughter's care, I was going to have to manage my own self and my own physical and mental health. That was an incredibly tall order.

I had to do the impossible and make it possible. The thing is, the situation with my daughter as it was a few years ago—and continues to be—is exhausting. Add in the demands on a daily basis of being a business owner, and some days, I just want to crawl under my bed.

So, how did I do it? How do I STILL do it?

I'd be lying if I said it was easy. Or that every day is good. I'm sure it will come as absolutely no surprise when I say that there are a good number of days where I fake it until I make it. Not feeling like doing that interview? Put lipstick on and do it anyway.

Not feeling like building that website? "Sorry chica", I tell myself, "you gotta do it, because it needs to be delivered to get paid." Well, alright then. Nose back to the grindstone making pretty websites.

Maybe I'm feeling like stress eating? The temptation is real. But I know it's gonna make me really sick and probably give me gas and migraines. Not a winning combination. So that is off to the table.

In 2019, I decided to radically change my life, the life of my daughter, and really the lives of my entire family. In the period of a few months, I had weight loss surgery and got on the train to lose over 160 lbs. Then I got legal guardianship of my daughter so I could make sure she gets the care she needs, as well as disability, and a longer term hospitalization in our state psychiatric hospital.

While she was hospitalized, we turned the crank several more times, in crazy quick succession, with a lot of help from friends who stopped in to give me advice and help. We were able to obtain a neuro-psych evaluation and get her a slot with the North Carolina Innovations Waiver. Then in 2021, she was moved to a group home, right at the end of the pandemic once they started discharging patients.

While she spent time hospitalized, I spent working with my other kids and working on growing my business, with relatively fewer distractions including fewer psychotic calls.

But then she was discharged and the discharge planning had to happen. If you've ever been through discharge planning from our state psychiatric hospitals, let me just say it is what feels like a never-ending series of calls with social workers, doctors, carers, and all the things. Calls, calls, and more calls.

While trying to bring in clients, serve clients, and stay the course.

Left foot, right foot.

You might ask, *if it's so hard to have a business, why don't I just go get a job?* Some of my family have asked the same question. The answer is simple: with the sheer number of calls I get from my daughter, about my daughter, and never being able to predict when the next blow-up will happen; it makes it hard to be a good employee.

In fact, in 2023, I told my husband that I was thinking about applying to certain jobs so he might need to cover some of the incessant calls. He responded that I could take the calls from anywhere, no matter where I was traveling.

My daughter was hospitalized eight times in 2023, including about six months back at our state psychiatric hospital. Because of the nature of her illness, the first seven hospitalizations were the proverbial merry-go-round of trips to the hospital, then being discharged after some unspecified amount of time.

In fact, during her seventh hospitalization of 2023, I told them that she needed to go to Central Regional Hospital (CRH)—our state psych hospital—and they agreed with me. Still, they didn't think they could get her admitted. I told them she would get violent, as she had been showing a pattern of escalation of violence towards one caregiver in particular. They discharged her mid-day on a Monday, and by 9 PM that evening, she had stalked one of the caregivers at the group home, beaten and punched him, and jumped on him WWE style. She had to be restrained by multiple people and hauled back to the hospital.

I remain my own boss. Some days my boss is a b****. At least she understands that some days I need downtime or I need time to deal with calls about my daughter. It also means I am constantly juggling knives that feel like they're on fire.

Do I pay more attention to my daughter's needs today? Or my own needs? Or my clients? How do I balance it?

Truth is, there is no great answer. Some days I just wish I didn't have to wake up and deal with all the crap. It is never-ending. I know there will always be more calls, more stress, more trips to the hospital. Not to mention the needs of my other children, husband, even myself.

The trick is in getting up every day, getting focused on the things that MUST happen, and making sure that they happen. Every single day is a study in mindset. Checking and rechecking my mindset. Pulling my energy to myself.

Sometimes I have to take it minute by minute. My husband is a nice guy, but I've faced the reality that he is never going to step up and help out with our daughter. (And yes, she is his daughter too).

So I'm it. I am responsible for making all the decisions for my business, my health, and my daughter's health on a daily basis. It can feel really heavy. In fact, it usually feels massive.

I make a point of taking time every day to meditate, to focus on the good. I take time every day to focus on gratitude.

It can seem like it's never enough. Living my best life has never seemed so hard, and yet I remain determined to do it, because by beating the odds, keeping my daughter safe and healthy, and getting healthier and wealthier myself, I know that it's going to be amazing.

It already is amazing, if only because I decided that it is. It is a choice.

As I say regularly: "Let's do it!" Let's make it amazing.

Haley Gray

Haley Lynn Gray, MBA, is a business and marketing strategist, founder of In2itive Biz Solutions LLC, and a Duke University graduate. With a background in engineering, Haley specializes in helping small businesses grow through data-driven marketing and operations integration. Known for her commitment to delivering exceptional, ethical service, she provides personalized strategies that drive measurable results. Passionate about empowering others, Haley also mentors women in leadership and entrepreneurship. She balances her career with a strong focus on family, personal well-being, and giving back to the community.

SEEKING THE ELUSIVE HEART

David Vine

I feel like crickets are jumping up at me, and life is dragging me down. I feel like a hazy cloud is floating by my eyes and a million thoughts are going through my mind every single day of my life. This is my life going through a sea of emotions day by day. This is my life.

I am forever seeking something; whether it be answers, love, a force of motivation or even notions of desperation.

Where do these feelings come from? You can say that over the past five to six years, life has always surprised me. Ever since the pandemic I have been drawn to something, maybe answers to my own questions.

This is my story of mental, emotion and physical instability.

It has been just about two years since my road accident in 2022. It's been two years of hell. At least that's how it feels. I have endured sharing my story around this moment for a good while now. Sometimes it feels like re-opening of old wounds and other times it feels therapeutic. Going through the endless trauma of hospital visits, doctors appointments, surgeries, and only just recently going through a bout of pain and haziness in my left eye. So you can say I'm partly visually impaired too.

To give a brief rundown of what happened, I was crossing the road in the suburbs of Helensvale, Australia. You could say the little green man (pedestrian light system; green for walk, red for stop) wasn't working properly, there I was walking across the road, all of a sudden I lost my footing, and slipped face forward smashing my face on the curbside on the side road. I looked like a zombie from the Thriller music video by Michael Jackson. I cracked my wrist in 2 places, damaged my spine, broke my nose and lost a lot of sensation in my right leg which has left me not being able to walk properly. That's the general gist of it.

After having countless panic attacks, night-terrors, nightmares, and triggered moments in public related to my accident, my psychologist confirmed and diagnosed me with PTSD. I literally cocooned myself. As far as life in general, I couldn't do anything, even just a simple moment of trying to make a cup of tea, it just wouldn't work for me as my wrist and legs were always shaking. A lot of people in my life just didn't get me, "Why are you having bad dreams?", "Why can't you walk out of the house?"," Why can't you cut the grass or cook dinner?" My legs were so bad that I literally couldn't get up. Once all the doctors and hospital chaos started, I was literally in a state of delusion with panic and anxiety attacks.

The accident changed everything. The once vibrant and independent person I was now a shadow of his former self haunted by the relentless echoes of that fateful day. The smell of asphalt and the screech of tires still filled my nightmares, leaving me trembling and sweat-drenched. The world outside my home had become a minefield of triggers.

That's how I felt for a long time. Emotionally I was a wreck, but I knew that this PTSD was going to be a part of me for the rest of my life.

I was forced to adapt to a wheelchair to go to medical appointments, and also needed a mobility chair for the shower. I was literally fearing the worst. Am I going to be like this forever? The first surgery I had was to correct my wrist. I needed a metal plate implanted just to be able to keep my wrist from flopping about all the time. The other crack in the wrist had to heal naturally as it was in the bone, a tiny chip, in other words.

My nose couldn't be operated on, that had to heal naturally.

All of the moments I was facing in terms of adversity weren't doing me any good. No one really knows what PTSD is until you experience it yourself. It's definitely not a feeling. You read stories all the time about soldiers coming back from war. War in anyone's mind is what you call trauma. These veterans lost loved ones, an eyeball, legs amputated from these horrible atrocities. This was a trauma to them.

I have looked into what mental health is. So how do you define mental health?

It is a person's condition with regard to their psychological and emotional well-being.

State of mind is important to everyone. A lot of people just see it as another excuse as to why this person is looney. That is far from the case. There are 4 types of Mental Health disorders;

- Mood (whether people affected in a depressive type of way through to Bipolar)
- Anxiety disorders (they can affect the way you react from day to day living)
- Personality disorders
- Psychotic disorders (such as Schizophrenic)

Everyone is complex in their own way. I have come to accept who I am as a person a lot over the past 18 months. You learn a lot too. The day I was told I am Autistic level 2 was kind of a relief. Like a huge weight was taken off my shoulders. Now people are looking at me and seeing me differently. I want to be labeled differently too. You really can't expect every person to be different, being the same is boring. If every person in this world was the same, the world would be a boring place. That's how I see the challenges that come along with it.

Over time my accident remained a traumatic event for me. It was always stuck in an endless loop in my head. I would literally wake up in the middle of the night with these and other terrors, huddled up crying. It was not a nice feeling. The ongoing nightmares are stuck on repeat all the time of the road accident. Till this day now, I'm still getting them. I knew I had PTSD from when they first started, but getting it confirmed by a psychologist was like a real life nightmare that I was struggling to get out of. My family was my rock most of the time, but also they just didn't understand how bad it was at the same time.

For this I'm seeking closure!

What matters to me most is getting past the adversity I experienced. As I see it, where there is trauma, there is the adversity we must overcome to get over it. Building resilience, and then learning to accept life is truly moving on, regardless of what you had to go through to get to that point in your life.

I do know now that as I soon come up to the anniversary of that fateful day, a few tears will be shed as a part of the shadow of my former self. I have the greatest support people around me, they have always been there for me. My Dad and my loving children, for that I know that will always be a part of me, and I love them very much for being that pillar of support and rock for me during those traumatic days.

I have done some reading on PTSD, and it appears to be a lifetime sentence.

But people from the community, people who knew me, were reaching out. "David, I haven't seen you in a while". Hearing those words saddened me so I felt I had to open up. Just talking about your feelings can really help. Even writing about them can help. I know I will never really get truly better, but I do know that if I continue on this right path, I know things would help me in my mind. It's a long recovery process. I'm trying and dealing with this ongoing pressure every day. Persevering to greatness, to the point that I know that one day I will really truly get there.

As I lay my heart on my shoulder I know that there are good people out there who are willing to help. I don't need to go seeking answers any more as I know my answers are within. Those are the matters of my heart!

Seek the heart and you shall find it. I did and I found it through the people that care about me the most, my family, my friends and my beautiful support crew.

I found my heart!

HERE IS A NEW STORY TO SHARE

Since this year has started in 2024, I felt that I was bound by societal pressures that I wasn't good enough, especially coming from outside sources that were crippling my mindset. You know that feeling when you have lost a piece of your heart. Well, it literally broke me and I was left in a sound of my own silence with no one to turn to. This was the first time I felt alone. I was hated on by certain people and I felt like I was the pariah of society, and I cried the nights away. I do admit I was supposed to have external support that was there for me in a sense, but nothing could compare to the absence of your own heart. One day I will really tell the real full story, but right now I'm in a position where I can't even contradict or fabricate a story on my own behalf. Its like I felt, "I'm damned if I do, and I'm damned if I don't," in the words of Bart Simpson.

I was a broken man, so the only place I could solemnly declare my solitude was sitting right in front of me: the online world.

I felt raw and lonely. I would literally turn to any one that was willing to listen. I tried the dating apps but they didn't work as you have to be willing to spend some time in order to even communicate with someone which was annoying to me. I even tried to be brave and go to a speed dating event, but never felt the slight pull of someone that could even be interested in me. Fat chance, I reckon?

But it wasn't till I was exposed to talking to a few women on Facebook that it really opened my eyes. You could say for a point that it could even possibly work, but low and behold, I was scammed rotten. So that never happened again.

Am I really doomed to the point of living the life of a lonely person? But who knows? No matter where it comes from, I am willing to open my arms and heart to maybe one day, find someone that will capture my heart again. It's not the fact of finding someone that will keep me strong, but I have felt I might have found it, in the people around me, the people that care for me, and the strong network of very good support workers that are there for me. Seeking the heart can mean a lot of things. People do matter, and the heart will follow.

David Vine

My journey from Brisbane, Australia, has been rich with diverse experiences and accomplishments. I began my fascination with technology early on, starting with games on the original Atari and advancing to the Commodore 64. This early exposure sparked a lifelong passion for both computers and writing.

After graduating from Kingston State High School in 1993, I pursued my interest by studying a Diploma of Information Technology. His career evolved over the years, encompassing roles as a business owner, self-published author, and entrepreneur.

My love of writing flourished in various genres, including non-fiction books focusing on business and empowerment, anthologies, magazine contributions, and fiction.

My collaborative efforts as a co-author include works like "Business Warriors: Taking Care of Working Women in the 21st Century," "Lessons I Learnt: Stories of Courage and Vulnerability," and his personal project "Building Resilience ~ Overcoming Business Bullies."

I have marked a significant milestone in my writing career, achieving Amazon Best Seller status in a number of categories for collaborative projects such as Letters of Love: A Collection of Uplifting Letters across the World, They are Magic Anthology, *and* Ascension Vol 1. Stories of Rising into your Soul Path and Purpose.

I have continued to evolve personally and professionally. I have found inspiration and growth in relationships, love, and personal development. I have expanded into new realms, including explorations into erotic literature, showcasing my versatility and willingness to embrace new creative challenges, as I now enter the world of getting my books into a physical bookstore by opening my own retail shop known as Story Time Books & Merch.

https://www.amazon.com.au/Its-already-yours-adversity-suc-cess/dp/1387378147/

SEEK THE HEART

SEEKING GOD'S HEART

Kelly Fritz

The sounds of car doors shutting echo through the air. I step back and take in a full breath of ocean air. I am excited.

"Today is the day that I will see a whale!" I shouted, announcing it to the world

Jen, my friend looking surprised, answered, "April is not whale season in Oregon."

I replied, "We can't put limits on a limitless God." You see, I'd had a God download. A direct download from God. Sometimes when this happens, it's instant faith. 100%. There are no thoughts leading up to the thought. It just is. Today I will see a whale. Whoo-hoo. Growing up in rural Montana left no moments at the sea-seeking whales. However, today was the day.

Have you ever just called it, said it, or asked God for something without even a glimmer of doubt? 100% faithful that I would see a whale, I continued to walk with Jen and the other girls who were with us for our weekend beach getaway. I joined them along the shifty sand and rocky ledge of the ocean. I stood at the top of the ledge gazing at the wonder of His creation, fully ready to see God's display of His vast creature like the one from the story of "Jonah and the Big Fish."

The ladies took off to gallivant around the beach, a celebration of freedom from our families for just the weekend. I stood and took in the scene. Orange hues at dusk, the breeze warm and inviting, off in the distance the sun about to make its great escape to night, and a storm coming in from the North. Sun beams shown through it. Lifting up my camera, I capture the scene waiting for the whale to make his appearance, even imagining the wave of his fin as it comes up and then descends like the sun under the water for his food.

After taking countless photos of the water and the stunning sunset, no whale appeared. Slightly devastated, but unshaken, I spent the rest of the weekend loving our trip and enjoying our time together. When I returned home I was excited to show my family the photos of the sunset. While looking at the pictures I called Cassie, our daughter, over to sit next to me to look at them. While I moved through the photos she said, "Look at the fish-shaped cloud!" I moved the computer closer to me.

I looked at what she was pointing to and yes indeed; there it was: my whale. A whale shape in the sunset clouds. This had appeared and disappeared right before my eyes, and I never saw it. I had the expectation that God would show me a whale in the water, and He showed me one in the clouds instead. This is my God, big, grand and always a surprise. Leaning back I took it in. My whale story.

I became very secretive of my photos after that. It felt like the creator of the universe was talking to me. Little old me. Honestly, it has scared me a little too. It would have been one thing for the whale to swim up, do its flip with his fin and swim off. This seemed so much bigger. A story to share with the world. How do you share this with a world that this God, this big God loves us so much?

My husband was the first one to question me on my secretiveness with my photos. He said that it seemed to him that I was not really sharing them with anyone. How can you when I felt like the God of the universe was talking to little old me. How do you share such a momentous God with a world that gets so offended by Him? That is when I negotiate what's going on with God. Yep, you read that right. I negotiated, saying I felt that what was going on was just so big. I thought this story may scare people. What if we bring it down a few notches and I just start tracking the hearts that God makes out of nature? Cloud hearts, puddle hearts and hearts in bird poop. I will take a photograph, I will not Photoshop them, I will just crop it and document it. I will look for your love and document it for the world. That is when I got serious and started looking for God's love everywhere, seeking the hearts that He makes.

The fact that I have dyslexia may be the reason I can find the hearts so easily. Early on in my search for hearts I would find them in onions, puddles and in the petals of flowers. Although reading and writing is very difficult for me having this disability. It was almost like a superpower seeing the hearts just stick out to me.

When I was young—about 10—I went to summer camp. Coming back home I got my camera film processed and I only had flowers and plants on the film. MY family got mad at me. Who goes to camp and comes back with plant pictures? However, now looking back I wonder, did I see something then, did I already track God's love and hearts in His creation? When they made fun of this hobby I stopped doing it. That light got squashed out of me. It was not until that April day so many years later that I was able to recommit to tracking and documenting God's creation and love for me and you.

I took a break from God when my best friend was killed in a car accident. I thought at the time that I was supposed to stop it. I was mad at God for not giving me enough information to stop it. You see, I have very vivid dreams, and all that summer before her death I kept dreaming of a funeral. It was like God was preparing me for what was next. After it happened, my anger over not being able to stop it took over, and I walked away. What brought me back was in my most desperate moment, praying for peace. That is like a direct call to God. It was a hard break up, my heart shattered, I needed God.

This 12 year break from God took me to some dark places, but now with a new found hope, I decided it was time. I was on my life quest of seeking God's love notes to the world and documenting it. It was easy. All I had to do was stay present when I was looking.

No depression, thinking of the past, no anxiety or worry about the future. Just being here now. Clouds, leaves, shadows of flowers and heart puddles filled my camera phone and Facebook feed. Soon I had people sending me hearts that they found. Still not sharing my whale story with the world.

After some time, I decided to make it more of a scavenger hunt with God. Asking for a particular heart in a particular way. "God, can I have a leaf where the colors in the center of a heart are green? The outline is colorful." The hunt was on. Every opportunity I would take to hunt for this leaf. On the crisp fall morning stepping out on my walk looking for confirmation of my request. God says that we should only ask and it will be given. However, the time between the ask and the receiving is in God's hands. Our faith must see us through. I looked, on sidewalks, in bushes, leaves floating on puddles or dancing down the road swept up by the wind. I was a faithful present observer waiting to see God's love.

One day about two weeks into this Fall leaf love hunt, I realized that I may not find this heart this season, and it may be many seasons that I would have to wait to see it. Shrugging off the timeline, and continued to forge ahead, looking every chance I got.

Then it happened a few days later walking along my usual route and no other leaves around lay one perfect leaf directly in my path laying down on the sidewalk. I stopped, stunned at first that I found it. Bending over and picking it up I let out a laugh. You see, God did give me a heart on this simple leaf, but He did it in reverse order of my request. The heart was colorful and the outside was green. It was as if God said, "Kelly, thank you for looking and asking for such a specific item, but I'm not Santa. I'm God and I will still have my will in this." Immediately I ask, "Who should I give this to?" Holding the leave in my fingers turning the twisting it in adoration.

A flash of a woman who regularly walks her Scottie dog in our neighborhood came to mind, like a still polaroid image. I was off on the mission to find her. Just two blocks and to my left I saw her. I waved at her like I was waving down a New York City taxi. She was out on her regular synchronized walk. Crossing the street, I announced to her that I had a gift for her. I quickly retold my adventure to find this love note and how great God is. I handed it over to her. These love notes are not just for me, they are to share.

On my love note adventure I have also learned that God can re-create the hearts that He has for us. Ever present, always looking, I had just arrived at the beach for a retreat 12 step weekend to help me overcome food addictions. I reluctantly went out in the pouring rain to my car to grab my bag. Reaching my hand to grip the door handle I saw it, a small water heart puddle just waiting for me to document. Pulling out my phone to snap a picture, just then another rain drop hit it and it ran off the handle to the ground. I got angry at myself for not moving faster to capture it. Standing there looking at the handle, I realized I could just ask God to make another one. "God, can you make me another puddle heart?" With the faith of a mustard seed I stood there looking at the handle with anticipation of the creation of this heart with the drops of the rain.

Out of the corner of my eye I see a group of people headed my way. Standing still staring at the handle of the car and not looking up, they got closer. Wouldn't you know it, the car they decided to get into was parked right next to me. Feeling nervous of what they may say or do about me looking at the door handle waiting on God I almost gave up, and went off, getting my bag and heading in.

Then God said "Are you worried about finite minds, or are you willing to spend some time with the creator?" With that I knew, of course, I would spend time with the creator. The world around me started to disappear with each second that I ignored the finite minds. They got in their car, backed up, and drove off, all while I stood in the pouring rain staring at the door handle waiting on God to make me a puddle heart.

Then on cue it was like time slowed down. I started to see the tails of the rain drops as they came down from the sky. One, an elongated drop hit the door handle , then a second drop with an almost longer tail landed. Then the last hit. There was a tiny love note. I snapped the photo quickly and thanked the Lord. Opening the car door the drop ran off the handle. I grabbed my bag.

Not knowing how long I had been gone, soaked through but content as a heart hunter, I went into the community room. My friend Julie looked at me soaked and asked "Where did you go?" Taking off my wet gear, with a giggle in my voice. I said "I had to spend some time with God." In these small moments with God, I wonder what else we could ask for, and if we just were willing to wait, what we would receive. Maybe, as His creation, He longs for the connection with us daily. These small acts of looking for His created love notes keeps me ever present with Him.

The other thing that I have noticed with this heart hunt I'm on is that I can find many of them, new every day on the same old walk I do. I have not changed my path, yet I seem to find so many new hearts each day. One early afternoon I decided to go out on my walk. However, this time when I got to the end of the sidewalk in front of my house I asked God, "What way should I walk?" Standing at the end of the sidewalk waiting for God to let me know. He is no longer a pillar of fire in the sky at night or a cloud by day, the Israelites wailing in the desert in Exodus, but He is the same God of yesterday, today, and tomorrow. Does He take joy in the fact that we consider Him in our day? Consider what way He may want us to walk. I stood and waited. Soon a small black bird flew to the right. That was good enough for me, and I was off.

I soon came to a yard with seeded out dandelions. If you were a seeded out dandelion hunter this was the yard to be in. I started to wonder if God placed a hidden heart here for me. I bent over and stepped on the green grass looking. I plucked one of these treasures, holding in my hand twisting and looking. No heart, just ready for a wish, I asked God.

"If I blew on this, would you release the seeds in the shape of a heart for me?" Closing my eyes and getting ready to blow a rush of guilt flooded me. With all the things in the world to worry about, cancer, famine, war, I'm going to ask the creator for a heart in a seeded out dandelion? Then a flash of a mustard seed came to my mind.

In the Christian faith, God asks that we have the faith of the size of a mustard seed. That small size would be enough. At times in my life my faith is either a mustard seed or a hot air balloon, or somewhere in-between, however, either way my faith is solid.

Eyes still closed, taking in a breath and blowing slowly on the weed, I opened my eyes, and there it was, the heart love note for all the world to see. Elated, I snapped a photo for me, my heart was documented, and I was off again. Asking God again.

"Who should I give this to?" These moments when I'm so connected to God, I feel like it's a high, Like I'm John the Baptist from the Bible, with honey in my hair running around the forest wrapped in sackcloth. I came to a couple standing and talking and I just knew it was not for them. I moved quickly to my neighbor's house, went and knocked on the door.

Birdy, their daughter, answered the door.

"Hello," in her sweet voice.

"Yes, yes, is your mom home? I have something for her."

"Hold on one moment."

"Kelly, how are you?" Birdy said with a smile.

"Birdy, Birdy" looking at her almost out of breath of excitement of what I received.

"I have something for you." Re-telling the story in I'm sure was hurricane wind speed, I finished and reached out my hand holding the love note wish to her and said, "This is a gift from God." She graciously took it. Looking at me with wonder.

"That is so strange."

"Strange?" I say to her.

"Yes, I just spent the whole morning picking dandelions for dandelion tinctures." Just like that it was wrapped up. She had spent the morning working on what I just brought her. What a delight that God did this for her, reaching out, speaking to her in her dandelion language.

"You keep it, it's special." Hugging her I walked off full of God's love. That is how this works. In order to find the heart-shaped love notes in His creation you have to be present and looking for Him. If you are willing to do that He will unveil a full world of expression of love to you.

He does this daily for me, multiple times. I have been taken way out off the beaten path following my GPS in my car just to discover a giant heart shaped puddle bigger than my car. Sometimes I argue with Him and remind Him that I have to get to my appointment on time. Then He gently reminds me that he controls time. Ha! Well, with that Lord, you are right.

I have had moments where I feared I would not find a heart. Like when the seasons change and my morning walk is in the dark, then I spot a shadow from a streetlight hitting a leaf and there is the heart shadow. Another time I did not find one on my walk, but when I got home and cracked open my egg, I found the heart in the shape of the yolk.

Even during illness and injury when I was unable to leave the house to go on my heart-hunt walk. He showed up in the leaf of a get-well plant, or a red raspberry in my food, or when I cut open an onion. He found a way to reach me. This is a deep longing love that He has for us.

Lately I have discovered that His love runs deep. That when I take the time to look for it and find a heart, If I take a further moment to look within that heart, whether it's a puddle on a leaf, or a snail I will find hearts within hearts within hearts. You see His love for us runs deep. My dyslexia I'm sure helps me see hearts better than others. As I share my story of overcoming my depression and anxiety by looking for God's love, people share with me that they either know someone who is a heart hunter too, or that they find heart rocks, or I will get photos sent to me of hearts they find and then thought of me. That brings me such joy! I'm sure God loves this also. Any time we consider Him in the world of turmoil I'm sure He delights in us.

A few years ago I was even able to do a small art show at a local café showing off all my heart cards. Capturing the photos I have been able to share them with others in canvases and cards that I have made. I take them to bazaars and writers' conferences to continue to share how God shows up daily in my life.

These love notes are a lasting reminder of the love He has for me. Even now I get so excited when I find a new one, I giggle. It still feels like a lovely scavenger hunt with me and God. I cannot tell you the number of times that I find a heart in a purple onion. At this point it's weekly.

Do you ever think that you are missing out on something God is trying to show you? Remember we cannot put limits on a God who has no limits. Sometimes all we need to do is ask. Matthew 7:7 "Ask, and it will be given to you; seek, and you will find; knock, and it will be opened to you."

NOTE: All Bible verses are taken from the New American Standard Bible.

Kelly Fritz

Kelly Fritz lives in the picturesque state of Oregon with her beloved husband, Keith, her stepdaughter, Cassie and her husband Tim. Despite living with dyslexia, she has cultivated a passion for writing, weaving together both fiction and non-fiction narratives that inspire and captivate her readers. Her work is deeply influenced by her strong connection to God, which serves as a guiding force in her life and writing. Through her stories, she aims to share the beauty of faith and the power of perseverance.

TAKING OFF YOUR TRAINING WHEELS

David Hollingsworth

"I'm NEVER GOING to ride a bike!"

My 5-year-old son, Jamie, yanked off his helmet, threw his bike down and ran into the house, crying loudly. I had been trying to teach him to ride for about a month, and no matter how hard I tried, he kept falling over. Even with training wheels, he couldn't keep his balance.

For most kids, riding a bike is a normal rite of passage, with many of them picking it up easily. In Jamie's case, however, it was much more difficult—he had no sense of balance. He wanted to ride, but for some reason, he just couldn't balance long enough to get rolling.

Remember when you first learned how to ride a bike? When you climbed onto your bike, put your hands on the handlebars, feet on the pedals and gave yourself a push? You probably wobbled a bit and fell a time or two, but after a while, you found your sense of balance. You felt like you could go ANYWHERE you wanted to go, because once you got in motion, there was no stopping you!

That's what Jamie wanted. To feel that wind on his face, the sun shining down, the sense of speed and freedom that comes with learning to ride.

Jamie was a bright, happy little boy, but two years earlier, we received news that would permanently change his and our life's direction. He was right on track with a lot of developmental milestones but had trouble with some motor skills, especially with emotional regulation. After a few visits with his pediatrician, we were referred to a developmental specialist, who performed a battery of assessments. After the appointment, they called us in to give us the results.

At the appointment, the doctor waved us into the conference room, and he gave us a stack of reports that looked about the size of a doctoral thesis. Clearing his throat, he looked us in the eye.

"I'm not going to mince words here", he said. "Your son has several challenges that are going to take a lot of intervention and work for everybody involved." He paused to see if we grasped the seriousness of the situation before continuing. "He has some communication and language delays. He exhibits repetitive movements, like rocking and flapping his hands. He has sensory sensitivities to sounds, smells, and tastes, and trouble with emotional regulation and meltdowns if he gets upset. In addition, he has trouble learning complex physical movements and fine motor skills."

"In short, your son has Autism."

We sat there for a moment, trying to absorb everything the doctor said, and the implications for Jamie.

The doctor kept talking, but after a while, the words just seemed to blur into each other. He painted a bleak picture of what Jamie's future might look like. He said that Jamie may never go to a regular school, graduate, or hold a job. He may even struggle with normal childhood activities, and because he had no internal sense of balance, Jamie may never learn to ride a bike.

Remember when you first learned how to ride a bike, how hard it was to balance?

Imagine what it would be like if you couldn't balance at all.

Imagine the dreams you had for your child – all the hopes for them running, playing, making friends, and having a 'normal' childhood – all those disappeared in an instant. Instead, we had to start thinking about limitations, obstacles, and things that Jamie might not be able to do.

Jamie didn't care about what the doctor had to say – he just wanted to ride his bike.

Jamie wouldn't give up. Every day, I'd come home from work and Jamie would run out of the house, all excited, "Dad, I wanna ride a bike!" He would climb on his little red bike with training wheels, hands on the handlebars, feet on the pedals, and I'd give him a push.

He'd wobble a bit, then fall down.

He'd get on the bike again. And fall down. He'd try over, and over, and over. Jamie just couldn't balance, even WITH his training wheels.

Eventually, Jamie would get frustrated, tears rolling down his cheeks. "I'm never going to ride a bike." He'd run back into the house and slam the door.

As a parent, it tore my heart out.

Jamie really wanted to learn how to ride; I wanted to find a way to teach him.

But how?

I remember back when I was FIVE years old, I had trouble learning to ride a bike. I had to look to someone older and wiser, who already knew how. I thought I had the perfect teacher. It had to be my brother JIM. Jim knew how to ride a bike, right? Jim knew EVERYTHING! Jim was SEVEN!

Jim "borrowed" my sister's Schwinn bicycle, and took a long look at it. He said, "These training wheels just slow you down," and took them off. He convinced my sister that we'd only have the bike for a little bit, and that everything would be just fine. He also assured me that we'd be very careful, and that I wouldn't have to worry about anything at all.

THEN he took me and my bike to the top of the tallest hill in the neighborhood, put my hands on the handlebars, my feet on the pedals, and gave me a PUSH.

Once I got in motion, there was no stopping me.

Literally. I kept picking up speed, going faster and faster. Trees started to blur as I accelerated down the hill. I kept looking in front of me, frozen in fear with a death grip on the handlebars. I ran right through a stop sign at the intersection, and towards a family having a picnic in their front yard. They turned towards the siren-like wail getting closer and closer, thinking it was a police car, but in reality, it was a 6-year-old screaming at the top of their lungs. At the last second before impact, I closed my eyes and hoped for the best.

I heard a sickening CRUNCH, as the front wheel of the bike lodged itself into the wheel well of their '64 Buick, which was parked in their front yard, at the bottom of the hill. Once I realized that I wasn't dead, I slowly opened my eyes to the family crowded around me. They helped me pry the bike away from their car. The dad said, "I think you'd better head home, son."

As I walked my sister's bike back up the hill, I had a realization: it isn't balance that keeps you upright, it's MOTION. The bike has to be moving FORWARD, FAST ENOUGH to GIVE you that sense of balance.

That lesson came back to me, and I wondered, *HOW do I create that motion, that sense of speed for Jamie? WITHOUT pushing him down a hill?*

To teach Jamie how to ride, we had to deal with a lot of issues in different areas. He had difficulty with gross motor and fine motor skills. We worked with many resources to build up his muscular coordination and dexterity. We helped him work on building strength and flexibility. Every skill he learned, from bouncing a ball to swimming influenced other areas of his life. As his skills improved, his ability to balance got better.

Jamie had difficulty tracking things visually. Another challenge was his inability to filter out audible and visual noise. We worked with a specialist to help Jamie better deal with visual inputs, and how to focus on specific things while ignoring others. We learned how to deal with getting services through advocacy organizations and working with therapists, schools, and behavior specialists to help him learn how to deal with frustrating situations. It didn't eliminate all problems but helped Jamie manage them better.

Because Jamie's brain worked a little differently, he had trouble regulating his moods. We worked with his doctors to identify medical and behavioral interventions that could make it easier for Jamie to deal with the frustrations of daily life. Over time, we had to make lots of changes; we found lots of things that didn't work. But during that period we found a few things that did, so we focused on those, even if those changed over time.

I had been reading about the physics of balancing on a bike. The way a lot of us learned was counterintuitive to the actual mechanics. When many of us learned how to use training wheels, we would lean AWAY from any feeling of falling. Instead, riding a bike is a constant state of falling forward. The faster you are moving forward, the easier it becomes to maintain your balance. When you use training wheels, you spend most of your effort trying to balance in place. To gain balance, you have to be moving. The faster you move, the more the gyroscopic forces keep you upright.

I remembered my brother Jim's words: "Training wheels just slow you down." So I took them off.

THEN, I bolted a handle on the back of the bike, so I could GENTLY steady Jamie while he picked up speed and learned how to balance.

The first day, I convinced Jamie to try again. I told him, "I won't let you fall." I walked behind him, holding on to the handle, and only adding support when I needed to, instead of constantly forcing the bike back to center. Jamie struggled at first, but he started to relax more while he pedaled.

It seemed to work! Jamie started to gain confidence in his ability to pedal, and as long as he kept looking forward and propelling the bike, he seemed to balance by just moving forward. After the first practice, I excitedly told him, "Jamie, you made it to the end of the driveway!" That may not sound like a lot, but I had been working on just getting started for almost two months. I had to help Jamie focus on moving forward and trying new things, instead of his previous failed attempts.

After a few days of working with the handle, and guiding him forward, he started to go a little bit further. By the end of the week, I was amazed. Jamie was able to ride a little bit further every day. Instead of just making it down the driveway, I was able to say, "Wow, you rode to the end of the street!" His confidence kept improving, and his enthusiasm grew even faster. Jamie was riding without training wheels, but I was still holding on. I didn't want him to fall or get hurt, but really I was holding him back. I didn't want him to get discouraged or hurt himself while learning, but for Jamie to learn how to ride, I had to learn to let go.

Everyday throughout the summer, Jamie would ride just a little bit further. He'd pedal along and say, "Hang on Dad!" I'd hold on to the handle and yell back, "I'm hanging on, Jamie!" as I'm running along behind him. But every day, I held on just a little bit less.

By the end of the summer, Jamie was riding around the block. Jamie's pedaling along. He'd yell out, "Hang on Dad!" and I would still run along behind. But by that point, I wasn't hanging on at all. At the end of the block, Jamie got off the bike, "Were you hanging on, Dad?" I struggled to catch my breath.

"Jamie, I haven't been hanging on for a week. That was all you."

Jamie got a BIG grin on his face. "Dad, I CAN RIDE A BIKE!"

I was proud of Jamie that day, and still am. Jamie went from riding a block, to riding a mile, to riding five miles, and when he joined Boy Scouts, he signed up for the Cycling merit badge. He learned the mechanics of how a bike worked, how to do basic maintenance, and how to ride in a group. We'd ride along with the group on longer and longer rides. We did two 10-mile rides, two 15-mile rides, and then two rides of 25 miles. For the final part of the badge, we had to do a ride of 50 miles. Early one morning, the organizers took us to the start of a local bike trail and started us off on the trek.

Less than two miles into the ride, a participant stopped short, and Jamie crashed into the back of their bike, sending him off the trail. He had a couple of scrapes on him, so I asked, "Are you OK?" thinking that this might be the end of the attempt. I feared the worst, but he quickly got up and brushed himself off. He climbed back onto the bike, gave me a thumbs-up, and said, "Let's do this."

I breathed a sigh of relief, and we rolled out. We rode up and down hills, learned to ride in a group, and kept moving forward. A few hours and rest stops later, we rolled into the Belle Haven Marina on the banks of the Potomac River, completing a full 50-mile bike ride. He earned his Cycling Merit Badge, and it was hard to forget the smile on his face, but the smile on mine was probably even bigger.

Jamie had come a long way from his first attempt at riding a bike. It took a full two years to get to this point, but it didn't end there. We went from a 50-mile bike ride with the Scouts to a metric "century" of 100 kilometers (62.5 miles). We'd ride 3-4 times a week, and during the summer, we'd plan out rides of even greater distances. The following summer, we did a full 100-mile ride as part of Maryland's Seagull Century, taking in the Eastern Shore, Chesapeake Bay, and Assateague Island. The first time we tried the full 100-mile ride, Jamie would ride along behind me, while I fought the wind in front. After the first rest stop at 22 miles, Jamie got on his bike and started to ride ahead of me. He said, "I'll meet you at the next rest stop."

When I got to the next rest stop, Jamie was nowhere to be found. Even though the ride was well supported, with lots of signs and traffic support at every intersection, I wasn't sure if he was still on the course, and contacted the ride officials to start looking for him. I still hadn't located him by the 45-mile stop, and I was beginning to worry that he might be lost—so we got the police and safety personnel to put out an alert—because he might be lost.

I didn't see him at the 65-mile rest stop and was considering abandoning the ride to look for him, but took the chance to ride on to the last stop before the finish at 80 miles, just in case. I rolled up to the stop, and there, by a tree, was Jamie, sitting in the shade. I asked him if he was OK, and he said, "I'm tired, but I dropped you like a bad habit, didn't I?"

Relieved, I sat down with him to take a break. I asked him if he could finish the ride, and he said, "I don't know, I'm pretty sore." I said, "Let's find the support van and get a ride back." I checked with them and told Jamie, "We can get a ride, but we have to wait an hour before they can go." Jamie threw a leg over his bike, and said, "Let's do this." I told him to stay closer to me this time, and about 90 minutes later, we rode across the finish line, completing the full 100-mile ride.

Since then, we've completed four full century rides together. But it didn't end there.

That victory spilled into other areas of Jamie's life. The confidence he gained from learning to ride started giving him the confidence to try more challenging goals. While we were able to take advantage of some special education support, Jamie graduated high school with a standard diploma and a 4.0 average.

He not only learned to ride a bike, but I taught him how to safely drive a car. He's been driving for 10 years now, with a near-perfect record, and is a safer driver than most others on the road. He's taken trips of up to several hundred miles on his own, with minimal support needed.

In Scouting, Jamie went from Tiger Cub Scout, all the way to completing 21 merit badges and achieving the rank of Eagle Scout. He received two flags that had flown over the US Capitol and the Pentagon to commemorate the occasion. He received letters of congratulation from his U.S. Representative, Senators, and the President of the United States.

After graduating from high school, Jamie enrolled in college, and with support from his peers and other programs, completed his Associates degree and continues to learn as an adult.

One of the biggest concerns we had for Jamie was his ability to live on his own. As parents, it's one of the things we worry about most. Who will take care of our children when we are no longer around? Once he completed his degree, I started researching programs that could help him live independently.

There was a lot to learn. I had to find out about how to find housing, how to qualify for benefit programs, and how to keep Jamie engaged because he also had a strong need to feel that he was contributing to his own independence. I worked with financial advisers to set up a Special Needs Trust for him when I was no longer around, and modified my estate plan to make sure that any inheritance he received down the road wouldn't disqualify him from the services he received.

I found out about Medicaid Waiver services that could support his independence, and housing support programs that could allow him to live on his own with the level of support he needed. We were able to find a program that allowed him to have his apartment. He has an aide that comes in a few times a week and helps him clean, but he takes care of all of his meals, shopping, laundry, and daily care. He drives himself to his volunteer work and medical appointments. He picks up his prescriptions and manages his medication. Essentially, he does almost everything for himself and is building his community to build an independent life.

Living with Autism is challenging, but having lived with it through Jamie, I've learned that everyone has challenges, and everyone has gifts. While Jamie has difficulty navigating new relationships and may struggle with complex human interactions, he's surprisingly empathetic and has great chemistry with animals. Since he was young, he's loved dogs and cats, but especially dogs. He grew up with a Boston Terrier that bonded with him and helped him learn empathy much better than any human could have taught him.

He's got an affinity for 'smush-nose' dogs, like Bostons, Pugs and French bulldogs. When he sees one, he'll ask the owner if he can meet the dog. He'll get down on their level, and interact with them in a way the dogs seem to love. To this day, he's got great chemistry with almost every dog he meets, and I believe they've been an important part of his growth to independence.

Today, he's living on his own, still picking up speed, riding into his future.

It all started with taking off his training wheels.

Once he got in motion, there was no stopping him.

What about you?

Have you been too dependent on YOUR training wheels?

Are you feeling stuck, like you're not making progress?

Have you gotten started, made it to a certain point, but holding on to your safety net has been holding you back, keeping you from picking up speed and going where you really want to go?

Your challenges may not be the same as Jamie's. He taught me we all have challenges, and we all have gifts. It's important to identify what challenges are out there, how to meet them and work through them. It's also important to recognize your own unique gifts and strengths. We all have unique areas that make us the individuals we are, and by recognizing those strengths, allow us to give those gifts back to others.

We can be stuck in one place by being afraid to share those gifts, because of a fear of failure or rejection, but like my brother Jim said, "Training wheels just slow you down."

You've got to grab life by the handlebars, look ahead, and give yourself a little push, because without moving forward, you're bound to fall down, and not make ANY progress. Once you get in motion, it's a lot easier to change direction, if you find you're not headed the right way.

Sure, you may wobble a bit, you might even fall down! But moving FORWARD will increase your sense of balance, and you'll go ANYWHERE you want to go, and there will be no stopping you!

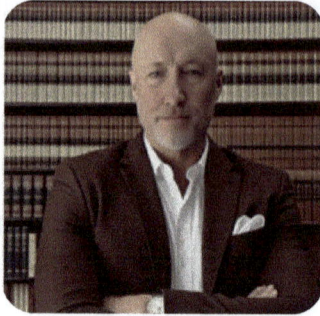

David Hollingsworth

David Hollingsworth is an accomplished IT executive and technology expert, award-winning speaker, storyteller and author of the book, Get Out the Door!

With over 25 years of IT experience, David is a proven leader in effective solution architecture, winning proposal development, IT service delivery, and operations. He has an MBA from Xavier University, and multiple industry certifications, including PMP, CISSP, ITIL Expert / Managing Professional, and SAFe Agilist. David has expertise working in both commercial and Federal sectors, including global consulting firms, DoD, Federal Civilian, and Intelligence Community environments.

David speaks on achievement, resilience, goal-setting, overcoming obstacles, and service excellence through his engaging humor and personal storytelling. He leverages his technical and professional background to provide positive steps to career advancement, and his speaking and storytelling experience to connect with the audience and leave a lasting impression.

As a spinal injury survivor, David came back from a devastating motorcycle accident in 2004 to run up the Empire State Building, completing two triathlons, the Assault on Mt. Mitchell bike ride, and the Marine Corps Marathon — all in the same year.

FROM MESSY MIS-STEPS TO HEALING THE WORLD WITH LOVE & LAUGHTER

Elaine Williams

In August 2000, I moved from Austin, TX to NYC. I got sober at the same time which, by the way, I don't recommend. But hey, that's how the universe rolled with me. Now that I was sober, I thought, "Finally! Smooth sailing from here on out." Spoiler alert: it wasn't.

I've always had a tendency toward magical thinking, believing things would just miraculously work out. I didn't realize just how twisted my thought patterns were, how much trauma I had been through, and how much healing I needed. But ignorance can be bliss, right?

I believe the universe, God, or whatever higher power you call "her" gives us grace. It's grace that we don't know how hard things are going to be, because let's face it, if we did, we might never start. If I had known how challenging it would be to pursue acting in NYC, become a stand-up comic, or even manage being a landlord, I might have chickened out. I'm so grateful I didn't.

Why am I sharing all of this—my missteps, my messy, over-committed life—with you? Because my mission is to help heal the world with love and laughter. And guess what? I can't do that without you.

As I write this, I've been sober for 24 years. I've made way more mistakes sober than I ever did while using drugs and alcohol. I want to share what I wish I had known back then, so you can make your own mistakes and maybe avoid a few of mine along the way. After all, life is just one big learning curve.

I've always been an action-taker. My problem was taking too much action without thinking things through first and then internalizing every mistake as if it were a personal flaw. Sound familiar? I've seen this same pattern in brilliant people everywhere—turning mistakes into self-criticism (or self hatred) and shame.

Let's break that pattern together, shall we?

Now, let's go a little Brene Brown and dive into shame. Oh, the joy! (If you don't know her, look her up after this chapter.)

My parents divorced when I was four, and my dad remarried a woman named Maria, a refugee from Yugoslavia with more baggage than a carousel at JFK airport. My dad was a dentist and, in true rom-com fashion, they met in his office. But he was also a pharmacist, just what Maria, who struggled with mental illness, needed in her life.

Growing up in an alcoholic family, I was told I was "too much." Too loud. Too fat. To everything. (Spoiler: I wasn't fat, just short and muscular.) Maria projected a lot of her unresolved pain onto me, and like the good little codependent that I was, I took it all on without question. I was told I was selfish, greedy, and (with the utmost disdain), "just like your mother." And so began my long, complicated relationship with shame.

Fast forward to college. By my junior year at UT Austin, I learned to channel all that shame into a productive little crystal meth habit. My roommates were losing weight by putting white powder up their noses, and I thought, "Hey, why not?" I had struggled with my weight for as long as I could remember. Maria put me on my first diet when I was in first grade, then I spent my life on a cycle of starvation, binging, and purging.

Meth seemed like the perfect solution and for a while, it was. But somehow, I realized the drugs were killing my GPA, so I dumped the rest down the toilet. After the meth, I read *Codependent No More* by Melody Beattie, and finally understood it wasn't my fault that Maria drank. I wasn't the reason for her addiction or our chaotic family life. I felt lighter than I had in years. I'd been carrying this tremendous weight that I didn't even know was there.

Fast forward to 2007.

I was hustling around New York City doing stand-up comedy. Tired of the boys' club, I thought, "You know what? I'll open my own comedy club for women!" Of course, that takes money, so naturally, I got into real estate. Because nothing says "empowerment" like rehabbing and renting houses, right?

It seemed like a good idea at the time.

I even took a real estate class to learn how to be a better landlord. Spoiler alert: knowing how to fill out a lease doesn't magically prepare you to manage a three-family house, especially when you are codependent and desperately want your tenants to like you.

SUPER TIP #1: If you hire a real estate coach, make sure he lives in the same country as you, and not, say, Canada. Just trust me on this one.

So there I was, buying a house in Philly that my so-called "real estate buddy" helped me rehab. By "help," I mean he gauged me, dragged out the project for months, and overcharged me. But hey, it looked good on paper! Remember it's 2007.

Then, I bought two more houses in East Texas because another "friend" said they were great investments. Did I do my due diligence? Nope. I trusted them both, because clearly, I thought I was living in a rom-com where everyone's intentions are pure and nobody cares about commissions.

SUPER TIP #2: Most humans have agendas. Just because you're generous and loving doesn't mean everyone else is going to be. (That was a fun lesson.)

The Texas houses were full of surprises. What one person calls a "renovated" house might actually just be a house with a bunch of Band-Aids on it. Also, when a home inspector tells you not to buy a house, listen to the man. I didn't.

SUPER TIP #3: Listen to the experts and do your own research.

I didn't realize the area where I bought my Texas houses has six prisons. Yes, six. Let's just say the local economy revolved around people working at the prisons or visiting family in them. Not exactly the bustling hub of prosperity I had envisioned.

One property manager forgot about one of the houses and squatters moved in for a few months, doing $10,000 worth of damage to the house I had just spent $25,000 renovating. It's funny now — ten years later, sort of.

Eventually, I sold both Texas houses at a loss. They came with battle scars, but I finally admitted defeat and let them go. My plan to flip houses? Let's just say, I was the one who got flipped.

I honestly think they would've turned around if it hadn't been for the worst timing ever. The global economic crisis hit. My big, brilliant plan blew up in my face. I was devastated.

Intellectually, I knew it was a global meltdown caused by the subprime market collapse. But emotionally, I was swimming in shame. I stopped trusting myself completely.

The worst part, I wasn't in touch with any of my real estate buddies. I was too ashamed to reach out. I felt so depressed.

My inner voice was on a loop:

"Why bother getting out of bed, Elaine? Everything you touch turns to shit."

I knew I needed help, so I found a good psychiatrist and started some meds, which helped. I wished I could've declared bankruptcy like so many others, but I was too proud. I didn't have the emotional bandwidth to even think about it.

Fast forward again to 2009 and my next big "oops" with real estate.

"Is this Elaine Williams?"

"Uh, yes, this is Elaine."

"Are you the property owner of 2305 Colorado St, in Philadelphia?"

"Yes."

"Did you know your house burned down?"

I paused. "I'm sorry, what?"

"Your house burned down. No one's been living here for months."

Oh. My. God.

The tenant that I wanted to kick out my property manager had talked me into allowing to stay. This tenant would pay just enough to keep the sheriff away and then stop paying again right away. We had to go through the arduous five month eviction process two times, because I trusted my property manager over my gut. I deferred to a man (an authority figure), even when my intuition was screaming at me! (This might be a theme in my life.) I just had my 2nd eviction process in Philadelphia with the same darn tenant when I got the call.

SUPER TIP #4: Listen to your gut, especially when it's screaming at you, even if it's an authority figure!

This same property manager assured me it was handled until the house caught fire. It seemed he had been stopping by to post notices but somehow missed the whole "burnt house" thing. You know, minor details.

The universe, however, sent me an angel named Greg Bogart. He helped me get the insurance payout and negotiate the rehab costs for after the fire. I had to fix the house (thanks to Philly's requirement to prove the renovation before releasing the money), but Greg found a contractor who got everything done fast and cheap.

The fire was a blessing in disguise. It cut my losses in half. Later, Greg's real estate buddy told me, "Elaine, you never should have bought this house." Ouch, but true. I didn't live nearby, didn't have a team, and was in way over my head. I finally admitted defeat, sold the house, and walked away.

So, what's the lesson here? No matter how carefully you plan, mistakes will happen. The quicker you can say, "Oops, this isn't working," learn from it and forgive yourself, then the faster you'll move forward.

SUPER TIP #5: Don't internalize your mistakes. Doing this for years almost broke me. I added a lot of meaning to things instead of being able to see them simply as lessons. Shame wrapped around me, like I was a failure, and sometime along the way I stopped trusting myself.

It took me a long time to realize that my mistakes do not define me. They were just part of the messy, imperfect process of learning and growing. Once I stopped viewing every setback as a personal failure, I saw them for what they truly were: opportunities to evolve. The hardest part was forgiving myself and trusting I could move forward, even after the most painful missteps.

If any of this resonates with you, reach out. Don't go through it alone. I spent far too long thinking I had to handle everything by myself. You do not. Whether it's shame, fear, or needing support, find your community. You deserve to shine and if I can help you spread your wings, I'd love to.

We're all in this together. Let's heal the world with love, laughter, and a lot less shame.

Elaine Williams

Elaine Williams is a video performance coach, keynote speaker, speaker coach, best-selling author, podcaster and comedian who has over a decade of experience working with entrepreneurs to build confidence and a captivating presence on camera and with public speaking to get their message out in the world with authenticity, ease and humor.

Some of her credits include: Saturday Night Live, America's Got Talent, HBO, ABC, NBC, FOX, The New York Times, Hay House Radio & the Huffington Post.

She's turned the messiness of early trauma, addiction and abuse into her message of resiliency, laughter and healing.

Her clients have gone from never doing video or speaking live to having their own YouTube Channels, doing International Book Tours, and speaking for NASA.

SEEK THE HEART

JOURNEY TO HEALING

HOW TRAVEL ELEVATES MY
MIND, BODY, AND SPIRIT

Karen Robinson

Once upon a night, in a land far, far away (Canada), a little girl dreamed of getting away from it all. The little girl was not born into a family of world travelers and didn't experience her first airplane ride until she was 19 years old! She scored a trip paid for in full courtesy of the University of Maine to attend a leadership conference. Was this the trip that hooked her? Nope.

I was the toddler who opened her arms to anyone visiting. Please pick me up. Please take me away. Where are we going? I didn't like being at home. It was dysfunctional, dramatic, and traumatic. I desperately wanted to escape and often stayed with my best friend Janet for overnights as often as her parents would allow. I didn't feel bored at her house. We would go places and do things! Janet's dad took us places, and one time we traveled on a small trip a few hours away to stay with Janet's relatives in central Maine for a few days. What an amazing trip for us back then!

I haven't been everywhere, but it's on my list.
SUSAN SONTAG

NEWBIE TRAVELER

I'm guessing my first trip was with my grandparents to New Hampshire to visit relatives there. I enjoyed my first road trip to visit my great aunt and uncle. Seeing new sites, eating out, and just being around people. My grandmother loved going to flea markets to sleuth out salt and pepper shakers. What a weird collection, I thought. We spent many weekends with her bargaining and hustling for the best deals for them only to be sold by my grandfather when she passed away. They gave her joy and a purpose for our wandering weekends so I guess they did indeed serve their purpose.

Most road trips, before I went out on my own, were sponsored by my grandparents or my aunt and uncle. My nuclear family never traveled. Ever. We never went to a single place or stayed in a hotel room together. Ever. As I write this, it is hitting me in such a different way. Do other poor and traumatized children want to travel as much as I did? I hated feeling trapped, isolated, and alone. Did I say I would go anywhere with anyone at any time? I mean it. Put me in a car with a few snacks and a good book any day! But let's stop and explore on the way. I prefer traveling with people who will let me plan the stops and adventures or who have places in mind. Driving long distances without exploring does not interest me nearly as much. These drives tend to be boring and put me to sleep. I want to stop and look around!

Road trips are the equivalent of human wings.
Ask me to go on one, anywhere. We'll stop in
every small town and learn the history and
stories, feel the ground, and capture the spirit.
Then we'll turn it into our own story that will
live inside our history to carry with us, always.
Because stories are more important than things.

VICTORIA ERICKSON

SHAGGIN' WAGON

My first really special long-distance road trip happened in our shaggin' wagon! My Aunt and Uncle purposely purchased a van for a road trip from the tip of Maine to Virginia Beach. We stopped in New York to see the Statue of Liberty during the summer after my 10th year of high school. Photos do not do her justice! She is magnificent and I can not imagine how immigrants struggling for entry into our country must have felt when they first laid eyes on her in her full glory. She is not a messiah, but seeing such a gigantic statue representing freedom and hope is powerful. After New York, our next stop was Washington DC, where we toured the Capital, the Vietnam Wall, The Washington Monument, the Lincoln Memorial, and nearly all of the museums. Looking back,

I can't believe how much we fit in so quickly. It was also my first time at Arlington Cemetery. What is crazy now, I live fairly close to Arlington and visit often.

We traveled on to Virginia Beach as my uncle's older brother was retiring from active duty service. My first military retirement ceremony. I didn't know then I would work for the military for over 16 years and attend multiple ceremonies. In high school, the ceremony seemed boring, but I fondly remember Julie, my uncle's niece, taking my cousins and I around the boardwalk and the strip. She was a young adult and very cool. It felt so much more exciting then the small town I grew up in. A wonderful example of how travel can be fun!

WHY DO I FIND TRAVEL FUN?

I embark on journeys to heal and rejuvenate. I discovered travel is the ultimate high for my mind, body, and spirit. From street markets in picturesque cities to the serene landscapes of untouched nature, every adventure I experience is a step towards wholeness. Join me as I share how wandering the globe not only filled my passport with stamps but also my heart with joy, my mind with clarity, and my spirit with a renewed zest for life. I'm completely serious when I share with you that travel has changed my life for the better. I believe my deep appreciation for travel started after being trapped in a dysfunctional, abusive home as a child. As an adult, I refuse to feel trapped by my past, unhealthy relationships, or toxic work environments. I choose to explore, run free, and be a fun-loving, relaxed girl all over the world.

Travel far, travel wide, travel deep.
UNKNOWN

138

LIVING OVERSEAS

Skipping forward 15 years from my first visit to Virginia Beach, I find myself in a miserable marriage. I didn't see it as running away at the time, but I was desperate to change my environment. Working for the federal government meant I could apply anywhere in the world for a career move. I applied to Japan and The Netherlands. Japan snatched me up first. My ex seemed conflicted but decided to come with me and our daughter. I remember thinking at the time it was an unsurvivable relationship.

I hate being right and we lasted a few months. Details are irrelevant at this point as he waved goodbye and left us in Japan, for the best, but very hard.

> *The world is a book, and those who do*
> *not travel read only one page.*
> SAINT AUGUSTINE

HEALING GRIEF

After my daughter's dad left Japan to return to the U.S., intense grief settled in for both me and my sweet girl. What could I do? I rescued my credit card from my wallet and booked tours throughout China. I spared no expense and planned a trip of a lifetime. My daughter and I traveled extensively in Japan and all over Asia. We lived in Okinawa, Japan for five years. Travel became our passion and we enjoyed every single moment of it.

My first time traveling overseas alone, I didn't feel fear, but I desired to keep us safe. Thus, I hired private cars to pick us up at the airports and this option was way more affordable than I anticipated! I neglected to hire a car in one location and regretted it. Who I thought was a cab driver started to guide us away from the airport and my intuition kicked in. I saw a police officer while in my best

Mandarin asked the driver, "Taxi?" He nodded. As I continued to follow the dude, he sped up when he saw the police. The police started yelling, "No!" and escorted us to a real taxi driver. OMG. The dude was just going to inflate fare prices, right? No kidnapping attempt, right?

Hong Kong thrilled us with Pandas, the night market, the views from Victoria Peak via tram over the harbor, and a short time at Hong Kong Disney. In Shanghai, we marveled over the Chinese Acrobats, the beauty of Yu Garden, and the awe of the massive Jade Buddha in the temple! She is reclining, massive, and gorgeous! I love the Bundt. We observed the traditional tea ceremonies at every stop! The tradition and ritual of tea preparation is a must-see if you haven't yet experienced it. A beautiful exercise of being in the moment, being present. Mindfulness at its best.

We explored the Forbidden City, Tiananmen Square, Temple of Heaven, in Beijing and climbed the Great Wall. Of course, we limited our walk because of the cold weather and the climb is super steep! We traveled to Xi'an to bear witness to the Terracotta Warriors. Seeing the ancient army in rows upon rows is a sight you must see. How cool to have your own gang of warriors be buried with you. Talk about robust protection! After experiencing the combat team, our tour guide delighted us with a trip to the theater for a dumpling show! The fun shapes of the animal dumplings - pure delight! The theater entertained and dazzled us. I dressed my daughter in a cute, little, silk, mustard-yellow kimono. Heart melting!

I will always treasure our trip throughout China. We hopped planes every other day and allowed the tours, landscapes, architecture, temples, and more to heal our broken hearts. The crisp weather, the exercise, and the nurturing food warmed and mended our hearts. We became hooked on travel! We went on to explore Japan, Taiwan, Korea, Thailand, Hawaii, Guam, New Zealand, Australia,

Myanmar (Burma), Malaysia, and probably a few other places I'm forgetting! I fell in love with the world. My daughter, at three years old, requested her passport and asked about gates, seat numbers, and blossomed on our adventures. She fed tigers, and a giraffe that was gross. The giraffe's saliva is thick, long, and extra gross! We helicoptered through glaciers in New Zealand and merged with scenic backgrounds on long train rides.

Now that you know some of my travel wonders, I want to share more about the benefits I experienced in mind, body, and spirit. Travel stimulates my mind, energizes my body, and comforts my spirit. I crave it and love how I feel when I get to explore cultures around the globe while taking a peek into how others live. I like seeing how produce and veggies look in the markets, and have you ever visited floating markets? So much fun to row your canoe and shop to your heart's content. I'm fascinated by how clothing is worn and how people drive. I seriously geek out on this stuff.

To travel is to live.

HANS CHRISTIAN ANDERSEN

HEALING MY BODY

At home, I mostly sit all day. If I have many Zoom sessions or meetings, I'm stuck in my office chair unless I have a client who prefers phone sessions. When those happen, I can sometimes get in a walk. When I travel, my mind is occupied with physical healing. I tend to get in more walking, hiking, and movement in general. Climbing and moving are amazing for our cardiovascular health, muscle strength, and improve overall fitness levels. I'm feeling more motivated just writing this. I want to enjoy my later adult years with improved mobility. Thus health and fitness at home and during traveling have finally moved up the value ladder for me. What about you?

Wellness is also more of a focus. I like taking deeper breaths, and maybe taking a nap! I enjoy checking out a spa to see how the soma is pampered. Have you ever been to a Korean bath or had a massage in Switzerland? If so, you KNOW what I'm referring to. If you haven't gone yet, be prepared for the lack of modesty, or the abundance of touchy-feely when the practitioners do their work. Now, I'm not talking about sexual activity, so remove those thoughts immediately. Of course, you can get those massages too - but I am not that kind of girl!

My body feels less tense when I travel. Getting away from my demanding job as a seasoned trauma recovery expert allows me an opportunity to truly let go and let my hair down. I think I can feel my blood pressure go down! When my stress is down, I can sleep better and allow my whole body to relax. I love getting extra vitamin D when I'm out in the sun, I like improving my bone health and I'm sure to cover up in sunscreen or my fair skin will burn to a crisp. Did you know travel can also boost your immune system? Apparently, fresh air and sunlight does our whole bodies good. Traveling simply makes you healthier!

I also feel nourished by other cultures' food. I love how fresh the food is overseas and how there are fewer preservatives and additives in the food. Have you ever watched "Somebody Feed Phil?" I adore Phil! One of my favorite things he says is, "I'm a passenger with my mouth open." Phil Rosenthal is comical; I love his facial expressions. Write to me and share your favorite episode! Healthrivedream@gmail.com. I love watching other cultures not only prepare food, but also how they present it. There is often great care and attention to detail. It all makes the experience more incredible.

In every walk with nature, one receives
far more than he seeks.
JOHN MUIR

HEALING MY MIND

Travel is not always easy. Sometimes my brain feels challenged trying to figure out where my gate is, and if I need to take a tram to get to it. Have you ever been assigned a gate at the very end of the airport? I have more times than I can count! It feels like I need to take a bus, boat, and train to get there. Excuse me, may I have a flight to get to my flight? Finagling transportation once I arrive, the logistics with hotel and meals, all of this takes some mental gymnastics, including the tour schedule. I take the details of trip planning very seriously. I want to see it all! I want to experience it all! Travel is healing to my mind as more often than not, I will take a break from technology and really allow myself time to de-stress. I allow myself to not think about work. In fact, I work very hard before leaving for a trip to make sure all clients have been seen and taken care of. Otherwise, I won't be able to fully relax.

As you may, I thrive when connecting with different cultures. This is how God created us, to be in connection with one another. Social connections make us feel like we belong, are valued, and have a purpose in the world. This also builds up our resilience muscles which leads to growth in all aspects of life.

Hopefully, you can see how meaningful traveling can be while on your healing journey. Expanding your mind and being more mindful is important for a new sense of renewal. Travel heals the mind by reducing stress, stimulating cognitive function, providing emotional release, promoting mindfulness, building resilience, fostering social connections, and offering a break from technology. These benefits contribute to improving my mental health, well-being, and overall life satisfaction. Have I convinced you yet?

Travel is fatal to prejudice, bigotry,
and narrow-mindedness.

MARK TWAIN

HEALING MY SOUL

Travel is soothing. Travel sparks gratitude. Even more true when seeing children begging on the streets, homeless around the world, the lack of nutritional food or clean water. How can one see this and not feel gratitude for what we have at home? We are spoiled and often ungrateful. Our complaints are often so small. I love seeing people smile and it seems the poorest among us have the biggest smiles and are the most generous. When globe trotting in New Zealand, the beauty of the terrain affirmed my beliefs in my Creator. Mountains, lakes, trees, and flowers all point to a divinity surpassing my understanding. Being in nature is peaceful and grounding for me. Especially if I'm visiting a beautiful garden or checking out older architecture.

I possess an appreciation of spiritual practices. This is called spiritual enrichment. When I open myself up to learning the tenets behind religious philosophies, it opens my mind and inspires me to think in new ways. This deepens my own spiritual practices and allows me to express a greater gratitude for my own faith. Did you know our faith walk directly influences our decisions and how ethically we move in our spaces? I love visiting temples, mosques, churches, and synagogues as they bring tranquility and a sense of serenity. I can feel God in these places. I love watching others pray and I honor their faith walks. Watching another pray is powerful. I can feel the energy and the oneness between us. I also feel inspired and can sense my own faith growing deeper.

Celebrating our different faith walks leads to greater inclusion and teaches us how we can learn to live and co-exist without conflict. Understanding more about religious beliefs, rituals, and philosophies, means there are fewer misunderstandings and prejudice. After all, most prejudice comes from ignorance or a lack of knowledge. To not be ignorant, I seek knowledge. I become curious. I focus on love and peace. It is okay if you are not religious, but please read and consider the beautiful messaging in these Bible verses:

> *Blessed are the peacemakers, for they*
> *shall be called sons of God.*
>
> MATTHEW 5:9.

> *If possible, so far as it depends on*
> *you, live peaceably with all.*
>
> ROMANS 12:18

> *But the wisdom from above is first pure,*
> *then peaceable, gentle, open to reason, full*
> *of mercy and good fruits, impartial and*
> *sincere. And a harvest of righteousness is*
> *sown in peace by those who make peace.*
>
> JAMES 3:17-18.

There are many, many more scriptures in the bible about peace. The same is true for all religious texts and most spiritual readings. Isn't it cool that travel can aid in us all being more peaceful? Travel contributes to peace by promoting cultural understanding, increasing our empathy, creating more open-mindedness, enhancing global awareness, shining a mirror on human rights, and environmental sustainability. Travel empowers me to want to do my part to build a more peaceful, tolerant, and interconnected world.

TRANSFORMING THROUGH TRAVEL

Travel broadens my perspective. I am fascinated by diversity - different customs, religions, rituals, and of course food. I like broadening my horizons and consider myself a global citizen. Anytime I am out of my comfort zone, it means I can be more present in the here and now. I'm not distracted by clients, paperwork, or my endless emails. I can be mindful and enjoy the beauty in front of me. At home, it is also hard not to be distracted by my laundry, the needs of my kiddos, and just noise in general. I feel my soul is joyful when I can explore, plan, and take in the beauty of other people, places, and things! I enjoy traveling alone, but also with family and friends.

Travelling is simply remarkable and it is fun too! I love its ability to heal my mind, body, and spirit, offering a holistic journey to my overall wellness. By reducing stress and tension, as well as encouraging us to be more mindful, travel rejuvenates! Exploring new lands close by and far away, fosters creativity and provides us with more emotional balance. Don't forget about the physical health benefits from increased activity, exposure to nature, and improved nutrition. It is easy to see how enhancing my overall fitness, health, mental health and spiritual well-being makes traveling a no-brainer for me. Spiritually, travel broadens our perspective as it is an opportunity to celebrate what makes us similar as humans as well as learning about our unique differences. Exploring our world encourages us to focus on self-discovery, and deepens connections with our neighbors across the globe. The word transformative gets tossed around a great deal but there is simply no other word in the dictionary to describe what travel means to me. Travel has transformed me and travel will continue to transform me, and hopefully you, into being the best version of ourselves.

> *Traveling—it leaves you speechless,*
> *then turns you into a storyteller.*
>
> IBN BATTUTA

Karen Robinson

Karen Robinson, MSW, ACSW, LCSW, CCTP-II, is a best-selling author, speaker, therapist, transformational coach, podcast host, and trauma recovery expert with 25 years of professional experience. As the Founder and CEO of Heal Thrive Dream, LLC, Karen leads a mother-daughter company dedicated to empowering trauma survivors. Heal Thrive Dream's mission is to empower survivors to heal from past wounds, thrive in their relationships, and create dreams for their futures. Karen's extensive expertise is underscored by her certification in Complex Trauma, making her a leading authority in the field.

https://healthrivedream.com

SEEK THE HEART

PAUSE, PAMPER, PROSPER

Donna Palamar

Do you ever wish you could just run away from all the chaotic pressures and responsibilities of daily life?

Just for a few days at least?

The tension keeps building up. It seems unbearable and you wonder which end is up? Yet, you keep thinking, "If I could just push through, things will calm down and I'll get a break."

You multitask like a pro and keep all those plates spinning. You think "I'll finish this project and then things will be easier for a while and I'll catch my breath." Surely, sooner or later it will all even out.

You rush around to meet deadlines, being pushed and pulled in all different directions, thinking you're making everyone happy, keeping "them" on track, making them look good, and keeping everything looking like it's running smoothly.

What about YOU? What do YOU need?

What price are your life and health paying as day after day goes by and you're STILL on that hamster wheel?

What is your tired, overworked self, telling YOU that you need?

When do YOU get time for YOU?

Do you dare be so selfish as to feel or think you could take the time to regroup and hit the reset button on everything?

It seems reasonable to be all caught up in the minutia and more than necessary as you rationalize it and make it seem tolerable because you know how important it is to you and others. You justify it by saying that someday, one day, you'll have time for yourself, especially since you put so much time and effort into all these areas of your life, you'll get that much-needed and deserved break.

I thought so too but never made the time for me, and because of that, I found myself exhausted, empty, and bankrupt in every sense of the word. At that point, no amount of tears could resolve my situation, no amount of wishing could take me back in time to make better decisions, and no amount of yearning could fix all the broken pieces. If only I had just taken a break, this could have all been avoided. I didn't listen to the warning signs when thinking I could do it all. It was draining the very life out of me. I pretended not to see the red flags when my sleep was affected and no amount of it ever seemed enough. I was waking up tired and wasn't feeling rested. I went from task to task with urgency and the days blurred into months and I had nothing really to show for it except bags under my eyes and a flabby middle from all the snacking and eating on the go.

Stress was causing my health and productivity to decline.

By this time, I needed to find a way to put myself back into the equation of a busy life and be able to not only survive it but also enjoy it and have it be manageable. But how? I'm burnt out, resentful, and overwhelmed. How do I get out of this tangle? Is there a way to escape all of this? What kind of legacy can I possibly leave behind?

When you're down, there's only one way to go, and that's back up. By being honest with myself, assessing my situation, taking a good look at reality, and realizing that I needed to reach out for help, I allowed myself the experience of getting what I needed. A time-out! Here's what I've found that has made all the difference.

CHANGE YOUR ENVIRONMENT.

Get out of Dodge for a while and away from all the who's and what's that are tiring you out. You'll find a new perspective on life once you're away from the everyday routine. You won't be running away forever, just a few days. You'll be back before you know it! Being in the space of other women allows us to learn and grow in ways that we can't or won't do on our own. We build trust and allow ourselves to receive guidance, friendship, and hope. We create bonds and are open to the possibility of keeping in touch and finding camaraderie in our quests to get the most out of life. Gather some girlfriends or join us on our next adventure and create some new memories as you use or rack up those frequent flyer miles.

DON'T GO IT ALONE.

It's great to take a time out, but you don't need to be isolated or excluded from others. There are plenty of like-minded women who understand your plight and who appreciate sharing an enriching experience while knowing that they are not alone in their feelings and situations either. Women are nurturers by nature. It's one of our greatest gifts. We can hold space for one another to speak our truth and not be judged as we find the acknowledgment that we so desperately need. We hear and see ourselves in others and this gives us a chance to look in that mirror and honor ourselves for what we have done and also look at the parts of us that could use some love, some kindness, some forgiveness, some slack, some encouragement, some grace and perhaps some tweaking. Be seen. Be heard. Be understood.

Don't have time or the budget right now to get away completely? Come join us online for one of our Pajama Parties for a few hours. Women from all over the globe connect and enjoy some pampering, fun, conversations, and activities.

TRY SOMETHING DIFFERENT.

Different perspectives and experiences can be so beneficial and allow you the very nurturing and revitalization that you so crave and need. Taking time for yourself is worthwhile and crucial in this day and age of uncertainty and tension. Are you open to treating yourself to a monthly Pause, Pamper & Prosper subscription box to enjoy in the comfort of your own home? Each month we have a different pamper box available to enjoy. Would you like one of your very own? Come check it out **Linktr.ee/donnapalamar**

What I found is that it IS possible to take some time away, to replenish myself, whether it's online in the comfort of my own home for a few hours or some time away for a few days. There's always a way. We have to fill our cup up first before we can pour it into others.

What I felt was deep gratitude for saying yes to this radical self-care that saved my life. I stopped the hamster wheel if only for a while, to be able to take care of my own needs and sanity in this crazy busy world.

What I learned is that it's necessary to use my own "oxygen mask" first. Once I reset myself, I feel rejuvenated and am ready to take on the world again in a healthier, happier way.

What I know is that what I need is essential. My needs matter. I don't need anyone's permission, and I don't have to apologize for wanting to enjoy life.

What I share is an invitation. An invitation to help yourself before you lose yourself. Before it's too late. Before you burn out, again.

Just in case you're still thinking that you can't because you do think that you need someone's permission, let me ask you why you don't have your own (permission that is).

Who said you couldn't have it? Shouldn't have it? Can't have it? Why?

Do you need it from someone else?

In case you don't know where to find it, I'm here to give it to you. Right here, right now. Are you ready? Here it comes:

> [*Your name*] IS HEREBY GRANTED FULL
> PERMISSION TO TAKE A MUCH-NEEDED BREAK,
> REST, TIME AWAY AND/OR TIME OUT TO BE THE
> FULL AND COMPLETE WOMAN THAT SHE IS.

I put it in writing. In case you missed any of that, doubt any of that, or think you can't remember any of that, you can get your very own copy of the full permission slip and statement at **www.Linktr. ee/donnapalamar** You can print it, frame it, laminate it, fold it and keep it in your purse, tape it to the bathroom mirror, whatever you'd like. It's yours. Your very own permission slip. Just for you.

The one thing I do suggest is that you use and enjoy it! In the meantime, try these permission activities on for size:

- Find a few minutes to get still and take a few deep breaths, a quick five-minute time out. If you need more, listen to a 10-minute meditation and relax your body and mind. You'll feel more able to get on with your day. If you need even more…

- Go take a walk to clear your head and get some fresh air. The movement can be invigorating and you can come back and complete your tasks. If you still need more…

- Have a pajama day and chill out. No drama, no deadlines, nothing but taking time out to regroup and re-energize. You can do this on your own, with some guidance from my specialized kits, or even by joining one of my online international pajama parties.

And if you need even more than that, find out what awesome retreat I have coming up. Book your spot whether it's for a week or a weekend, online or in person, and come join me for some much-needed connection to rejuvenate yourself so you can return home and enjoy life like never before.

The choice is yours. You can take the chance of keeping the pace at which you're going and risking total frustration, depletion, and staying worn out, or say yes to your health, sanity, and self-care to take a break for a while and exhale. You'll be so glad you did. I look forward to seeing you soon.

It's time to pause and pamper yourself so you can prosper!

Donna Palamar

As an international educator, author, speaker and empowerment coach, Donna helps women discover their power, honor themselves and recreate who they are so they can live fully.

She believes in transformative experiences such as retreats, events and subscription boxes. This allows the opportunity to restore & rejuvenate to surpass all that life brings your way.

Donna can frequently be found enjoying the journey of life, learning and the pursuit of dark chocolate with women all over the world.

ELIMINATE BOOM & SHOW THE TRUE YOU

Francine Juhlin

Life often presents a tug-of-war between the desire for authenticity and the pressure to conform. Many of us feel torn between staying true to ourselves and seeking acceptance from others. I, too, was trapped in this dilemma. I wanted to be seen but not entirely exposed. I felt different from the norm but still longed to blend in. This led me to wear a mask, crafting a persona to meet others' expectations. Behind this façade, I yearned to express my true self. Yet, after years of wearing these masks, I realized I had lost touch with who I really was. When I finally decided to unveil my true self, I couldn't find her.

This internal conflict between individuality and conformity is a deeply human experience, often rooted in a desire for acceptance and fear of rejection. The journey to balance these feelings can be challenging, but embracing your true self can lead to more fulfilling and genuine connections with yourself and others. The self-esteem required to balance these feelings and calm the internal conflict comes from deep self-reflection, often a painful experience when wearing a mask.

When experiencing the turmoil of conforming to others' expectations, we often have a pervasive inner voice—an intangible echo that reverberates within the corridors of our consciousness. This voice is not rational. It does not offer empirical evidence. In our quest to fit in, this voice becomes our guide, weaving its influence through our thoughts. However, its advice isn't always wise; it can either strengthen our resilience or, paradoxically, make us feel even more vulnerable.

In the intricate dance of self-discovery, we often find ourselves concealed by the veil of our own self-perceptions, unwittingly swayed by the insidious influence of a little voice known as BOOM—Bad Opinion of Myself. This irrational force, devoid of proof, thrives on our insecurities and fosters our worst instincts. As humans, we possess a remarkable adaptability that, over time, transforms BOOM's constant presence from novelty to mere background noise. Gradually, his nagging and put-downs cease to be questioned; they are accepted at face value.

Today, I am known as the Warrior Princess of Personal Change. As a change management specialist, I honed my skills in transformation within the industrial and corporate worlds. I helped employees navigate change and discovered how to make assembly line adjustments that saved time and money. However, when it came time to change myself, I didn't have a clue where to start. I just knew there had to be more to life. My self-doubt turned me into a worrier, too concerned about what people thought of me to show my true self to myself, much less the world.

Self-reflection wasn't easy because it required a deep and honest look at the layers of influences that shaped my identity. It took a lot of soul searching to realize that the condition I was in didn't develop overnight. Societal conditioning, family rituals, and biology all played a role in creating the version of myself that felt the need to wear a mask. Facing these truths meant unraveling years of ingrained beliefs and behaviors, which was both challenging and uncomfortable.

Growing up as an overweight child, I felt the sting of body issues acutely. My reflection in the mirror was a constant reminder of how different I felt from my peers, and this difference was often the target of cruel jokes and bullying. The snickers, whispers, and outright taunts etched themselves deeply into my psyche. Each insult was a blow to my self-esteem, making me more desperate to fit in, to be one of the crowd, and to be invisible at the same time.

When other kids were nice to me, I couldn't understand why. Why was one of the "cool kids" talking to me? As a rejected and conflicted child, I assumed it was just a joke or a prank. I wanted to be seen, but not really. I craved recognition yet feared it. I yearned to blend in, to find a place where I belonged, where I wasn't just the "fat kid." To achieve this, I put on a mask, shaping myself into what I believed others wanted to see. I became the joker, the peacemaker, the one who laughed along even when the joke was at my expense. Behind this façade, though, all I longed for was to be authentically me. Behind the mask, I was the wallflower wanting to be one of the cool kids.

The mask was a shield, meticulously crafted over the years, protecting me from further hurt but also concealing my true self. It became a part of me, a second skin that I wore so long I forgot what lay beneath. When I finally decided to take it off and embrace my authentic self, I was met with an unsettling realization: I couldn't find her. The years of pretending, of donning this facade to conform to others' expectations, had obscured my genuine identity.

It was as if I had been an actor in my own life, playing a role so convincingly that I had lost sight of the person I once was. The journey to rediscover myself was daunting, filled with moments of vulnerability and uncertainty, but it was also a necessary step toward healing and authenticity. As I peeled back the layers of pretense, a transformation began to unfold.

Each small victory in reclaiming my true self ignited a spark of confidence and self-worth. Embracing my imperfections and strengths alike, I found a renewed sense of purpose and direction. This transformation was not just about shedding the old, but about nurturing and growing into a more resilient, genuine, and empowered version of myself.

During my childhood, I was overweight, clumsy, and had an appearance that some might consider peculiar. My teeth jutted out prominently (later corrected by braces), and I had a unique facial tic (now embraced, not corrected)—my eyebrow that seemed to have a will of its own, moved independently in moments of its choosing. These characteristics set me apart from my peers in ways that I found embarrassing and challenging.

The combination of my physical traits and the reactions they elicited from others made me feel self-conscious and out of place. I often became the target of teasing and unkind remarks, which only deepened my sense of isolation.

I remember in the third grade, a kid put a tack on my chair. The tack affixed itself to the seam of my pants, never touching my skin. I heard snickering and chuckles around the room. Then the butt surprise specialist blurted out, "Her butt is so big, she didn't even feel it!" It took several minutes for me to understand what all the commotion was all about. As a result, I grew increasingly shy, retreating into myself to avoid further scrutiny and judgment.

In essence, my defense mechanism, while effective in reducing immediate emotional pain, also limited my ability to engage with others and experience the world openly. The weight of my insecurities (pun intended) and the barriers I erected around myself shaped my early years, influencing how I interacted with others and how I saw myself within the larger tapestry of my community.

Despite my shyness and ability to let my self-conscious tendencies rule, I have always loved to perform. From the time I was a child, I wanted to be on stage—dancing, band, singing, orchestra. I even tried acting. This overweight, clumsy, awkward child sucked at almost everything. But I excelled at music.

Behind my musical instrument, I found comfort and a place to perform while feeling protected. Starting in 5th grade and continuing to college, the tuba became my steadfast companion and my great shield. When I played the tuba, I felt a unique sense of safety and empowerment. Its large, imposing size was almost like armor, allowing me to hide behind it while still expressing myself through the music I created.

The tuba wasn't just an instrument; it was a sanctuary where I could channel my emotions and insecurities into something beautiful and meaningful. The deep, resonant tones of the tuba felt like an extension of my voice, a voice often silenced by my shyness and self-consciousness in everyday interactions. Playing music became a way to communicate and connect with others without the fear of being judged for my appearance or quirks.

I discovered a version of myself that felt perfectly aligned. Despite feeling big and clumsy in other aspects of life, behind my tuba, none of that mattered. There's a unique grace in seeing a little girl hauling around a tuba the size of a small car. In that moment, my awkwardness faded into insignificance, overshadowed by the powerful image of determination and passion.

I remember stepping out onto the football field for the first time. This arena was a place I would never experience as an athlete or cheerleader but being part of the band allowed me to share in that quintessential high school experience. After months of practice, my team, the marching band, played the theme from Superman and marched into formation with an "S" in the middle, just like a cape. The crowd roared. I felt as if we had won the national championship and that I had superpowers equivalent to Superman.

Throughout my school years, the tuba provided a structured and safe environment in which I could thrive. Band practice and performances were times when I could immerse myself in a world where my physical insecurities seemed to fade away. Within the ensemble, I was part of a larger whole, contributing to the harmonious blend of sounds. The camaraderie among fellow musicians fostered a sense of belonging that I rarely experienced outside of this space. The tuba was my faithful ally in the face of my lackluster athletic prowess. While others ran, jumped, and scored, or stood on the sidelines cheering for the jocks, I was perfectly content creating music and trying not to trip over my own feet.

At 18, I joined the Navy, leaving behind my beloved tuba. It was a bittersweet moment, as I closed the chapter on my musical sanctuary and started a new journey into young adulthood. As I sat on the airplane on my way to Navy boot camp, I knew it was time to reinvent myself and find another mask to cover up my insecurities.

The tuba had been my shield throughout my childhood and teenage years, a refuge where I could express myself freely and connect with others through music. Now, stepping into my new role in the Navy, I felt a mix of excitement and uncertainty. The Navy offered a structured environment like my band days, but with a different purpose and set of challenges. Although I had to leave the tuba behind, its lessons stayed with me, teaching me resilience and the power of perseverance. As I transitioned from the comfort of band practice to the disciplined routine of military life, I began to see how my experiences with the tuba had shaped me.

In the Navy, I sought a career choice that gave me the same feeling as being that little girl dragging the tuba so that people would see what I could do rather than who I was. First, I had to sell myself to the men I would work alongside. I needed to prove that I could carry my weight and contribute to the team. I wanted to earn respect through my actions, not just my presence. Back in the early 80s, women were not always given a fair chance because the boys felt like we were stealing their jobs.

After a failed attempt to integrate into the electronics shop, I felt hopeless. Then, I met my Petty Officer. He was the supervisor of the aircraft electrical shop and offered to tutor me. I was so excited for the chance to belong that I worked 8 hours a day in the tool room where I was assigned, then put in another 8 hours in the electrical shop. On my days off, he guided me through the manuals and patiently explained every detail of the systems we worked on. His mentorship was invaluable; he pushed me to ask questions, understand the intricacies of the job, and develop confidence in my abilities.

I remember one evening when I was eager to learn. The qualified aircraft electricians were grumbling about having to teach me, accusing me of trying to steal their "good duty." Determined to prove myself, I picked a job off the board. It was a simple task that I could handle without much guidance. After completing it, I asked how to fill out the required paperwork. One of the electricians flashed a smug smile and said, "Look at that, she picked the easiest job and still doesn't know how to sign it off." Just then, my officer stepped in. He scolded the lazy electricians, telling them that at least I had made an effort, and followed it with a string of words only a sailor could understand. After that, I became a permanent member of the electrical shop team.

When it came time to decide on a career, I wanted a job that challenged me both mentally and physically. I also wanted to stand out by doing something unusual. Looking back, this was another mask I wore to cover my feeling of not fitting in. While being an aircraft electrician was not inherently strange or unusual, in 1983, it was very strange and unusual for a woman in the Navy. I forced this round peg of a little girl into the square hole of the biggest boy's club in the world.

After 10 years in the Navy, I went to college to study electronics. There, I won the State of Mississippi prepared speech contest in the Vocational Industrial Club of America. However, I didn't place in nationals because I stood cowering my 5'2" body behind the lectern. The lectern was a symbolic mask, hiding my body image issues, hoping people would hear my words without seeing how I looked.

I hadn't thought about public speaking again until many years later. I joined a team dedicated to improving our workplace environment. Together, the team and I delivered training to every employee in the organization—about 4,000 people in total. I felt confident as an information delivery system. I was able to hide behind the words of training, again wearing a mask that hid my authentic self.

As one of the project managers of this team, the captain assigned me the task of starting a Toastmasters club for our employees. I had no idea what Toastmasters was at the time. I learned that Toastmasters is an international public speaking and leadership program. That assignment changed my life.

Do you get butterflies when you speak? That is excitement. But do your butterflies catch on fire, like hot molten lava? That's fear. What are you afraid of? I was afraid of being judged and not measuring up to my audience's expectations. I was afraid of uncovering the insecure little girl buried under the fat and behind the mask.

I've shared how I was self-conscious about being fat, awkward, and funny-looking. In music, I hid behind my tuba. In college, I hid behind the lectern. As a corporate trainer, I hid behind others' words. As a beginning Toastmaster, my butterflies were caused by trying to be what I thought everyone else expected me to be. I was afraid of rejection and judgment, of not living up to others' expectations. I feared that if I showed my true self, I wouldn't be accepted. I was a round peg who couldn't even identify the hole I needed to fit.

Starting the Toastmasters club marked the beginning of a transformative journey for me. It was a step into the unknown, a leap away from the security of my various shields, and an introduction to my true self. Through this journey, I learned that genuine confidence comes from embracing who you are, not from hiding behind what you think others want to see.

Even after losing 100 pounds, I still felt awkward. My voice, not powerfully motivating like those of other speakers, was another source of insecurity. Yet, I entered the Toastmasters contest season, determined to step out from behind my shield and add humor to my speaking, to complement my funny face and quirky voice. I shed weight, my mask, and left BOOM behind. Those butterflies were on fire, yet I felt compelled to push through the awkwardness.

To my surprise, I discovered that I could write a funny story. More importantly, I learned that I had the ability to motivate people to try new techniques in their speeches. What I had considered awkward and funny-looking for more than 50 years turned out to be what made me memorable to an audience.

Facing judgment was one of my biggest fears. Yet, by allowing my Toastmasters friends to critique me, I uncovered the Warrior Princess within. BOOM's voice was quieted by the supportive and positive feedback from my new peers. This process of stepping out of my comfort zone taught me invaluable lessons about myself—lessons I never would have learned behind my barriers.

Embracing my true self meant confronting painful truths and healing old wounds. It was about recognizing that the desire to fit in, while natural, shouldn't come at the cost of losing oneself. As I began to accept myself, flaws and all, I found that genuine connections with others became possible. These relationships were based on mutual respect and understanding, not on a need to conform.

I began to inspire others to ask themselves, "What lessons can you learn?" Encouraging them to step out from behind their shields, I urged them to uncover new nuggets of self-confidence and wisdom. These discoveries have the power to transform their paths, propelling their personal growth to new heights.

Through this journey of self-discovery and overcoming insecurities, I realized that being a role model isn't about being flawless or fitting a certain mold. It's about embracing my unique quirks and imperfections and using them to inspire others. My journey has shown me that true strength lies in vulnerability and the willingness to grow. Now, I strive to motivate others not by pretending to be perfect, but by showing them that their perceived weaknesses can be their greatest strengths.

My journey to balance these feelings was challenging, fraught with setbacks during the process of self-discovery. For me, it started with small steps: finding activities I genuinely enjoyed, surrounding myself with people who accepted me as I was, and gradually learning to silence the inner critic that echoed the bullies' words. BOOM was holding me back. Now, when BOOM creeps into my inner thoughts, I yell, "BOOM GO AWAY! I'M NOT LISTENING TO YOU TODAY!"

Today, I stand before you not as someone hiding behind a tuba, a lectern, or others' words, but as someone who has triumphed over insecurity and fear. My story is one of triumph. Overcoming BOOM and finding the power of self-acceptance and the courage to step out from behind the masks I created has not only changed my life but also the lives of everyone I encounter. Having the confidence to connect with the universe as my true self has a domino effect. Sometimes, a smile from a stranger is all it takes to change the trajectory of someone else's life. If I hid behind my mask, the world could suffer the loss of another smiling face changing the world.

After peeling back several layers of that onion, equating to chipping away at the mask, I decided to test out my ability to change the world. In the grocery store parking lot, I noticed the lady parked next to me appearing to have an argument with someone over the phone. I saw the frustration and dismay in her eyes as we both got out of our cars to head in to shop. She slammed her car door, muttering about a "no-good freeloader."

I flashed my biggest grin and looked her in the eyes. The tension that had scrunched up her attractive facial features melted away, and she smiled back. As we passed each other in the coffee aisle, she thanked me for helping her. She explained that approaching the situation with a smile when she got home could help solve the problem and save her relationship, rather than causing chaos for the whole family.

This experience deepened my belief in the transformative power of genuine connection. It showed me that even a small gesture, like a smile, can brighten someone's day and shift their perspective on life. I was reminded of the profound impact of my bond with Marty and how his words not only altered the attitudes of the electricians but also forged a sense of camaraderie that turned them into my aircraft electrician brothers. It reinforced the idea that authentic connections have the power to uplift, unite, and change lives for the better.

The journey to self-acceptance and authenticity is challenging but immensely rewarding. By peeling back the layers and revealing our true selves, we foster genuine connections and spread positivity. This, I believe, is the greatest triumph of all: the ability to touch lives and make the world a better place simply by being ourselves. Through this journey, I have found not just a voice but my true self. And that, I believe, is the greatest victory of all. The power of self-acceptance and authentic connection is transformative, not just for oneself but for the entire world. So, let us all strive to embrace our true selves, for in doing so, we not only change our own lives but also light up the world around us.

ELIMINATE BOOM & SHOW THE TRUE YOU
https://personalchangewarriors.com/

Francine Juhlin

After suffering from debilitating physical issues caused by life's stress, Francine Juhlin found herself 100 pounds overweight, relying on pharmaceuticals, and facing the prospect of medical retirement. She felt stuck, unsure where to begin making changes. Drawing on her studies and experience as an aircraft electrician in the military, a manufacturing engineer, and her advanced education in Business Management, Francine reimagined the tools and techniques she had learned to help ease her own personal transformation. As she began helping others, she realized that many of the blocks preventing people from realizing their dreams stemmed from negative self-beliefs formed in childhood.

This realization led her to a new path as a children's book author with Sparklefeathers and Princess Francy: The Magic Library. In the story, Sparklefeathers helps Princess Francy overcome her fear of being different. Sparklefeather's mission is to grow strong, confident children today so that we won't have to fix broken adults later. Now living in Florida, Francine is dedicated to inspiring children and families through storytelling, helping them embrace personal growth and self-discovery. Her goal is to empower children to overcome limiting beliefs and grow into their best selves.

SEEK THE HEART

LIVING IN SERENITY

Heidi Livengood

MEETING SYLVESTER AND THE FARM

When I was around four years old, I was the most energetic kid in our trailer park. I had curly, strawberry blonde hair and bright blue eyes, and everyone said I was full of life. Thinking back on that time, it's amazing to think how things have changed. One of my favorite people in the whole world was Sylvester, an older man who was always kind to me. He felt more like a grandpa than any-one else I knew.

My real grandparents, aunts, uncles, and cousins lived far away, up north. But almost every weekend, my family would squeeze into our car and drive to Sylvester's farm in the deep south of Georgia. Every time we arrived, Sylvester would be waiting at the door with a crystal dish filled with the sweetest candies. I loved the simple life on the farm and all the animals.

One day, Sylvester told me his goat had just had kids. I spent the whole day chasing the baby goats around the barnyard, and I quickly fell in love with them. But when I came back to visit next time, I found out all the baby goats had died. I was so sad and didn't know what to say. It was the first time I felt that kind of loss.

THE HEN HOUSE

What had once been a safe space quickly became one of my most vivid early childhood memories. My younger brother and I had just discovered the great mystery of where eggs came from, and we were thrilled to find them in Sylvester's henhouse. In our excite-ment, we turned the henhouse into the scene of one of the most epic egg fights in history.

When my father found the mess we had made, he was furious. He dragged us to face Sylvester and confess what we had done. I had never been so afraid of him before. At that moment, I realized my father could cause me harm, and it shook my sense of security. Sylvester stepped in and scolded my father for threatening to punish us.

For me, being punished for even the most minor mistakes was nearly a daily occurrence. This was the first time I truly felt my safety was at risk, and it made me see my father as flawed, not infallible. That realization left a mark on me, beginning a deep sense of insecurity and fear of failure that would shape much of my future.

FACING ABANDONMENT AND ABUSE

In the spring of 1987, my family moved into a beautiful split-level house on two acres of birch and black spruce trees. Every morning, I'd wake up and look out the big, octagon-shaped window to see moose standing in the marsh in front of our house.

As wonderful as our new home and life was, my life was turned upside down in ways I couldn't fully understand at the time. My mom left our family. She told me that I was the reason she was leaving, and those words cut deep into my young heart. For about two years, she was absent from my life, a critical time when I needed her most. I didn't know why she left or where she went, only that she was gone.

The things my mother told me, blaming me for her leaving, only added to the weight of the situation. I began to feel as if I was at fault for everything, believing that if I had been a better child, she wouldn't have left. These thoughts were too heavy for me to carry, and they began to warp my sense of self-worth. I started to believe that maybe I was unlovable, that perhaps I deserved to be abandoned.

Over time, I developed anxiety disorders, PTSD, and even suicidal thoughts. I was constantly on edge, living in a state of fear that something terrible would happen. The man my mom had been with was unpredictable and violent, and his threats were real. He terrified me to my core, and I began to suffer from selective amnesia, forgetting entire parts of my childhood just to survive the trauma. I didn't understand then that my mind was trying to protect me from the pain, but it left me with a sense of feeling lost, detached from my own life.

As my family prepared to relocate, my mother rejoined our family. It has taken decades to forgive the hurt, but I have grown to love her for who she is and the sacrifices she has made. Several years following my mother's brave escape from the grips of that man we learned that he had been arrested for the fatal shooting of his next lover's husband. When I heard the news, I was shaken to my core. The chilling realization that it could have been my father he killed hit me hard.

For years, I had lived with the fear that he might come after us, that he might find a way to harm us. My mother was called to be a key witness in his murder trial, which was instrumental in the eventual imprisonment for which he is now serving a life sentence. For the first time, I also felt a strange sense of peace. Knowing he was in prison and would never come near us again made me feel safe in a way I hadn't felt in a very long time. It made me feel secure and believe I could have a future without fear. I began to find my way back to myself, piece by piece, as I understood more about what I had been through and why it affected me so deeply.

The trauma of those years shaped me in ways I am still learning to understand. The anxiety, the PTSD, the suicidal thoughts — they all had roots in those early experiences of abandonment and fear. I developed borderline personality disorder, struggling with intense emotions and a deep fear of being alone. I felt like I was hiding, always afraid that something terrible was just around the corner.

A NEW BEGINNING: MOVING EAST AND FACING NEW CHALLENGES

In 1992, our family got a chance to start over. We moved from Alaska back to the East Coast, where my father found housing for us on a military post in Massachusetts. Living there felt strange — we were a large family in officer housing, even though my father was an enlisted soldier. It often felt like we were pretending to be something we weren't. I was 11 years old at the time, and it was also when my sister was born. After having three brothers, I was thrilled to finally have a sister.

Around this time, my parents became more involved in my health. I began seeing a nutritionist and dietitian, and my mom helped me track everything I ate. She taught me how to calculate my basal metabolic rate and monitor my calorie intake to try to lose the weight I had gained during puberty. My dad and I would go on 4-mile walks every day, determined to build healthier habits together.

The weather in Massachusetts was beautiful, and our walks took us past ponds and a golf course, which made this time feel special, but a punishment of sorts. But despite all our efforts, the weight didn't come off. I was around 5'2" and weighed 150 pounds, which worried my doctor and my parents. That summer, we focused on healthy eating and exercise, but I still couldn't lose weight. I started to realize that there might be an underlying issue, something beyond just diet and exercise.

During this time, I developed a love for genealogy. As I dug through family photos and records, I noticed a pattern. Even my great-grandparents, who lived in poverty in New England, were overweight despite working hard and eating whole foods. It became clear to me that something else was affecting my weight — something that simple diet and exercise couldn't solve.

THE EMOTIONAL IMPACT OF BEING OVERWEIGHT

Being overweight as a child was a constant source of pain. The daily walks with my dad, meant to make me healthier, often felt like punishment, reminding me that I didn't measure up, that I was different from other kids. Instead of feeling supported, I felt exposed, as if my flaws were displayed for everyone to see. The focus on losing weight made me feel broken, as though something was fundamentally wrong with me.

My parents, who I believed should have protected me, often voiced their concerns about my weight in ways that felt like criticism. Though I now understand they were trying to help, at the time, their words felt like they were highlighting my failures. I internalized their comments, believing I was unworthy, unlovable, and flawed. This harsh inner voice told me I wasn't good enough and made me incredibly self-conscious, constantly worried about how others saw me.

This mindset affected everything I did. I believed I wasn't good enough or pretty enough to be loved. Even my parents seemed to criticize me constantly, restricting what I could eat while my younger brother was allowed treats. My father would tease me about looking like my aunt, who had been mockingly called "Thunder Thighs" as a child. The only praise I seemed to receive was for my golden hair—which I was not allowed to cut. I began to believe I would never be attractive enough to marry or be truly loved.

Making and maintaining friendships felt impossible, as comments and teasing about my size were common. I lost trust in my peers and shut myself off from developing relationships, trying to protect myself from being hurt.

These experiences profoundly impacted my self-esteem, reinforcing all the negative thoughts I had about myself. Even today, as I work to build a healthier self-image, those early experiences still echo in my mind, reminding me how deeply words and actions can shape a person's sense of self-worth.

PHYSICAL, SPIRITUAL AND MENTAL INTERCONNECTED WEB

By my junior year of high school, the effects of my childhood traumas—abandonment, obesity, and a deep fear of failure—were taking a serious toll on my mental health. I was excited to take an advanced course in early American literature, a subject I had always loved. But as the class discussions unfolded, I realized that my understanding of the material was different from that of my peers. The teacher would ask what certain passages meant or what the author was alluding to, and my interpretations never seemed to align with anyone else's. This confusion grew more frustrating over time, and I felt increasingly isolated.

I was devastated when I received a failing grade for the second quarter. I hadn't received such a low grade in years, and it felt like my worst fears of failure were coming true. The fear that I might not graduate from high school weighed heavily on me. I felt trapped under the pressure of not being perfect, not being understood, and not being accepted. My depression deepened, and thoughts of suicide began to surface. I knew I needed help, so I asked my mother to schedule an appointment with my physician.

I sat in the doctor's office, still consumed by depression. I realized it wasn't just failing a class that was crushing me—it was the years of feeling belittled and emotionally abused. I simply couldn't take it anymore. The doctor, recognizing my distress, called my mother in and suggested I see a counselor. My mother quickly arranged an appointment with a psychologist, who also spoke with two of my brothers.

After several weeks of sessions, the psychologist conducted some initial screenings and diagnosed me with general anxiety disorder and dyslexia. In some ways, this was a relief. The diagnosis explained so much—how I had struggled in school despite my efforts. My dyslexia was so significant that the psychologist couldn't believe it hadn't been identified earlier. The anxiety was more familiar; I had experienced anxiety attacks since I was about nine, triggered by different situations and often accompanied by deep bouts of depression. At that young age, I had no idea what was happening or why.

Finally, having names for my struggles — dyslexia and anxiety — helped me identify the triggers that had plagued me for so long. I began to realize how many of these triggers were rooted in the traumas I had faced: the abandonment, the shame of obesity, and the constant fear of not being enough. While I still experienced episodes of depression, the diagnosis provided me with some tools and strategies to cope with my emotions day by day.

A NEW BEGINNING: FINDING MY STRENGTH

In the fall of 1999, I married my best friend. It was a bright moment in my life, a new beginning filled with hope. We decided to start trying for a baby, but it didn't happen right away. After a year of tracking my cycles and taking medications, I still wasn't pregnant. My religious tracking of fertility indicators was pivotal in my diagnosis of Polycystic Ovary Syndrome (PCOS). I felt like a failure like I was broken in yet another way.

But then, something amazing happened. With the incredible support of a doctor who was considered a quack amongst his peers, I lost ⅓ of my body weight. His treatment of my PCOS and hypothyroidism was successful. And, against all odds, I conceived our first child. It was a miracle, a moment of pure joy.

FACING NEW CHALLENGES AND CONQUERING OBESITY

With each subsequent pregnancy, I gained more weight until I reached 315 pounds at my heaviest. I had come to this point in my life where I felt completely helpless. I thought I had tried everything to lose the weight. Diets, medications and exercise did not seem to work no matter the level of dedication I consistently maintained. To get through everyday I soothed my emotions through eating. It wasn't until I was in my mid-thirties that I realized I had developed an eating disorder. All I had known before was that some people stopped eating as a way to gain control over themselves. I had no idea that the opposite could have been true. And for me that was true. I began binge eating to soothe my emotions and deal with and process these thoughts and that I was having. This had terrible side effects on me, emotionally and physically. All I could think of was food and it seemed like every moment of the day I was fixated on what to have and when the next meal would be. Eventually it got to the point where I was so unhealthy that I could no longer take care of my children.

At that point in my life I had six young children that needed their mother. My physical health had deteriorated so much that at that point I was bound to the couch. Each pregnancy I had developed sciatica but because of the excessive weight that I was carrying, my sciatic nerve was compressed constantly. I had begun physical therapy to try and fix that issue but I would be symptom free for only a day or two. Emotionally I was a wreck. You hear about those women that dislike how they look so much that they will not allow others to take photos of them. That was me to a T. It was time to make a drastic change.

I was in total despair about my situation and I didn't know what to do. I started thinking about the easy way out, ending my life, but the more I thought about it, the more I realized it would destroy my children and future generations. Having experienced abandonment early in my life, I knew the pain that being motherless created in a child. That was something that I could not even imagine doing on my own. This sparked my desire to seek other ways of improving my health.

I had heard about a controversial and experimental surgery being performed on people who were morbidly obese, so I started reading more about it. Eventually, I managed to schedule a consultation with a doctor. Being one of the first patients in Northern Alaska to pursue bariatric surgery, I had to jump through many hoops to prove that it was necessary for improving my quality of life. Over a year, I faced countless battles with my insurance company, consulted with bariatric surgeons in Arizona, underwent psychiatric evaluations, and had medical testing of every type done. Finally, in September 2010, I was cleared to have the Roux-en-Y gastric bypass surgery.

I thought losing weight would solve all my problems, but I was wrong. Instead, it brought new challenges. I realized I had deeply rooted issues with self-image and self-worth that I hadn't fully faced.

MY BIPOLAR DIAGNOSIS

This realization led me to another mental health crisis, but it also opened the door to true healing. I began working with therapists and engaging in healing prayer ministries.

This mental health crisis led me to some of the most amazing individuals I have ever met. I became deeply involved in healing prayer ministry for myself and helped other people through some of their past traumas. Taking part in the healing ministry brought up many judgments I held onto for years. Those feelings of not being worthy of love and being unlovable. Also, there are some hidden ones, such as feeling that my parents never wanted me. This was rooted so deeply in my being that it shook me to the core. I wept alongside others, and in those moments of being held, heard, and prayed over, I experienced a depth of healing that became the greatest gift of that season in my life. For the first time I was part of something larger than myself, a group of people that came together to help each other and share in God's love.

Having had weight loss surgery, I was aware of the risks and other associated disorders that may be a result. One thing that I learned about was how if you had an addiction associated with food before surgery. There's a high likelihood that individuals who undergo weight loss surgery may develop a substitute addiction. This often happens because we're still exposed to the same emotional triggers—only now, the original coping mechanism is no longer available. Many people who once turned to carbohydrates for comfort share stories of how that habit led to significant weight gain, which eventually brought them to surgery. Afterward, they experience a dramatic transformation—they start losing weight, feeling great, and reclaiming their health. But without addressing the emotional roots of their addiction, some find themselves trading one compulsion for another. They go to the gym and then they end up going to the gym multiple hours a day every day of the year. So they've traded one addiction for another addiction.

Being aware of these tendencies was very helpful for me because it gave me a little bit of insight into what I might be experiencing later on and how to deal with it. What I didn't realize was that the way that people saw me after I had lost a significant amount of weight would affect me and such a way that I traded a food addiction for an addiction that had extremely devastating consequences for my life. As I began to lose weight. I gained so much confidence I could go out in public and smile and I felt so good. People around me began to notice this and would comment on how great I looked. This affirmation happened so often that I internalized it and had moved away from being in a deep depression to the opposite, I became hypomanic.

During this time my life was very turbulent. I had moved to a new location. I discovered that the original bariatric surgery I had was not successful and was actually causing more issues and so I had to have a revision done. That revision was incredible as it really enhanced my quality of life. I finally was at my goal weight and it was time to move into the next phase.

So I sought help from a plastic surgeon to begin my reconstructive surgeries over the next couple of years. I underwent several surgeries to reconstruct my abdomen. My arms. My back and my breasts. I felt terrific and this gave me so much confidence, but it made me question my marriage. I did not feel as if I was wanted. This was one trigger that caused me to go into a very long hypomanic State. My marriage was falling apart and so my husband at the time and I began seeing therapists on our own but also marriage counseling. In addition, what I could not see was that my past traumas had come back to haunt me. At that time I received the formal diagnosis of borderline personality disorder as well as bipolar disorder. Having that diagnosis changed my life. For the first time, I felt heard. I knew that the depression that I had had in the past was not normal, but I couldn't figure out what was wrong. So I began intense talk therapy. I sought support from 12-step groups, began building my social network, and started therapeutic drugs.

REBUILDING MY LIFE AFTER HITTING ROCK BOTTOM

Although the new regimen eventually brought some positive changes, it wasn't before I hit rock bottom. My addictions had finally caused me to lose my home, my husband, and my children. I was at the lowest point I had ever been at in my life. My therapist, who was one of the most amazing women in my life, suggested I seek out other groups to gain support as the eventual divorce had alienated me from friends, church, and family. I joined the local Sex and Love Addicts Anonymous (SLAA) group and found strength in my faith and new friendships. I learned that I had to take control of my life, that no one else could do it for me. The first step is always the hardest. I admitted I was powerless over my addictions— that my life had become unmanageable. That was so true. The serenity prayer got me through those days. To this day I have the prayer engraved on my keychain.

The Serenity Prayer

God, grant me the serenity to accept the things I cannot change, the courage to change the things I can, and the wisdom to know the difference.

REINHOLD NIEBUHR

The decision to end my marriage was hard, but it was necessary for my growth and for my former husband's healing. As I continued to heal, I found new opportunities for joy and fulfillment. I started to rebuild my life from the ground up, focusing on what truly mattered to me.

LIVING MY BEST LIFE: LESSONS LEARNED AND HOW I CONTINUE TO LIVE MY BEST LIFE

Throughout the challenges I've faced—childhood traumas, battling obesity, and recovering from addiction—I've learned a lot about what it means to live successfully. The first step was realizing that change was necessary. The second was understanding that I didn't have to stay stuck in old situations. I had the power to take control of my life. Even when it seems like there are no options, being curious and advocating for yourself can open doors you never knew existed.

There are so many people out there who care about you, even when you might feel hopeless. Take a moment to reflect on your life and, even when it's hard, reach out. Community is one of the greatest gifts we have—whether that's through friends, family, faith, or professionals. It's okay to admit that change is needed and to seek help.

One of the things I continue to work on is eliminating negative self-talk. It's so easy to get caught in the trap of criticizing ourselves, believing those old lies that we aren't good enough. For years, I let that negative voice stop me from reaching my goals. But the truth is, we are capable of so much more than we think.

Another huge part of my healing journey was empowering myself through education. I learned about my body, my mind, and what I could do to live better. I joined online communities, reached out to professionals, and met incredible people who helped guide me along the way.

THE LESSONS THAT CHANGED MY LIFE

Some of the most valuable lessons I've learned along the way are simple but powerful. One is to fake it until you make it. Visualize the person you want to be and start taking small steps toward that vision. Each small victory adds up. The second lesson is to acknowledge how far you've come. It's so easy to focus on what's left to do, but don't forget to celebrate the progress you've made.

Setting realistic, attainable goals and celebrating milestones has been one of the most effective ways for me to stay motivated. Take each day as it comes and live it fully.

Here's what has helped me succeed:

- Advocating for myself
- Seeking help from professionals and my community
- Educating myself
- Setting and achieving small goals
- Cutting out negativity and toxicity
- Recognizing the challenges I've overcome
- Visualizing success, even when it feels far off

These lessons have shaped the person I am today, and I've never been happier in my own skin. I love the life I've built, and being the best version of myself benefits not only me but everyone around me.

HOW I'M LIVING MY BEST LIFE NOW

Every morning, I wake up with a sense of gratitude. I throw open the curtains and let the light in, even on days when I'd rather stay in bed. I remind myself to appreciate the second chances I've been given and the opportunities still ahead.

For years, I lived for others, which is important—but I was neglecting myself. Now, I'm focused on continuous improvement, on fostering curiosity, creativity, and growth in both my personal life and relationships.

I've reached my ideal weight by working with the right doctors and coaches who understand my body. Fitness is a priority for me, whether it's lifting weights at the gym or dancing like no one's watching. I cherish the time I spend with my family, especially as my kids grow and start to discover their own paths. My siblings, parents and former husband have accompanied me on this journey and I cannot be more thankful for their love and guidance.

In my career, I've been fortunate to build a network of supportive professionals, allowing me to thrive in ways I never thought possible. I'm also proud to be graduating with a master's degree, something I never imagined for myself, and I can't wait to use my education to help others.

I've found joy in hobbies like quilting, volunteering, pottery making, gardening and playing video games. I practice self-care, whether through massages or quiet retreats. I've discovered a love for travel, and some of my most exhilarating adventures have included swimming with sea turtles, riding camels on the beach, kissing the Blarney Stone in Ireland, devouring the best tacos in Puerto Vallarta and delighting in the most beautiful sunsets with my best friend. Next on my list: South Asia and the Nordic countries.

Building close friendships has been life-changing. I'm no longer fighting my battles alone. I have a supportive group of people who love me for who I am, and I'm endlessly grateful for them.

Living your best life isn't about perfection—it's about progress, taking small steps toward becoming the person you want to be. Remember that you are worth the effort. Reach out for support, stay curious, set goals, and celebrate every victory, no matter how small. You have the power to create the life you want, just like I did.

A CHALLENGE TO YOU

> *Your journey never ends. Life has a way of*
> *changing things in incredible ways.*
> ALEXANDER VOLKOV

I've faced my past and come out stronger on the other side. I've learned that the future starts today, not tomorrow, and that every day is a new chance to make life better. I challenge you to take charge of your life, to know that you have the power to create the future you want.

As St. John Paul the Great said, "The future starts today, not tomorrow." Every day is a chance to pave the way for a better future, to live with purpose, love, and hope.

Heidi Livengood

In this compelling chapter of her journey, Heidi Livengood shares the transformative story of reclaiming her health and embracing a vibrant life against all odds.

Living in San Jose, California, and raising six children, Heidi draws strength from her Catholic faith to navigate the challenges of spirituality, physical health, and emotional well-being. With honesty and hope, she shares deeply personal experiences that shaped her path toward living a fuller, more purposeful life.

Through moments of struggle, resilience, and self-discovery, she learned to redefine what health truly means—beyond mere physical strength, but as a holistic balance that harmonizes body, mind, and soul. With raw honesty and inspiration, she reveals the tools, practices, and mindset shifts that allowed her to transcend adversity, finding peace, purpose, and joy in the face of life's challenges.

This story of triumph and transformation is a testament to the power of perseverance and the courage to heal from within.

https://www.linkedin.com/in/heidilee2045

GRIEF HAS NO CLOCK

Katherine Kim Mullin

This is a brief glimpse into the darkest days I experienced, an emotional breakdown that left me broken with no explanation or apology.

I say the word grief and immediately it feels dark, like the feeling of being on a roller coaster, poised at the top of the mountain getting ready to fall. After all, the definition is sorrow after loss.

According to Kübler-Ross, a Swiss psychiatrist who wrote *On Death and Dying*, introducing the five-stage grief model, the stages are: Denial, Anger, Bargaining, Depression and Acceptance. She further explains the stages are not linear and all of them are not always experienced.

As I reflect on my life and think about these five stages which led to my own emotional breakdown, I will dive deeper into examples of how this model applied to the losses I encountered.

DENIAL: I had 13 miscarriages, and although they were losses, I denied the impact those miscarriages had on me. Another disappointment was I never got past that stage, I never recognized grief because I never acknowledged there was life terminated - I never held a baby. Another miscarriage, and disappointment filled with fear, were my only reactions. With what I know today, I say, "Hell yeah, I was grieving, and did I ever really get past it?" As you reflect on your life, I would suggest you take a closer look at the things that have happened, to recognize traumas that you might have simply denied. These can have long-term effects, beyond what you see or feel in the moment. Today, I know I never really dealt with many related issues until I healed from my emotional breakdown. I honor the loss my body and mind lived, and now accept and move forward recognizing the impact those miscarriages had on my life.

ANGER: I divorced and dealt with the betrayal, there was no denial there. It came from anger but I thought there was nothing I could do about it. So, I believed I accepted what I felt was an injustice. It made me sad and embarrassed. I felt not only a loss but a failure and shame. I am grateful that I moved on to find someone new and have a loving and harmonious relationship today.

BARGAINING: Wow this is a good one. When I learned my grandfather died, I was in denial, angry and hit this bargaining stage. The day after I buried my grandfather, I bargained with God that I would stop crying if... and that gave me temporary relief from the pain thinking one day I would see him, hoping he really wasn't gone.

DEPRESSION: I invested in a business, but there was a falling out that left me sad and feeling like a failure. I lost a substantial amount of money and time. I also lost a friendship, someone I loved, because I walked away, and that sadness was overwhelming. It stopped me from getting too close to anyone for a long time. I was afraid of getting hurt again.

ACCEPTANCE: I lived with this for many losses because I often went straight to acceptance, using this statement as a guidepost, "accept the things you cannot change." But I wrongly assumed that I accepted when it was only a coping mechanism. Acceptance is not a shortcut to bypass the grieving process.

I would suggest all these were parts of a coping mechanism that gave me temporary relief from the hurt I was feeling. All these instances left painful and unprocessed memories which were stacking up in the dark places of my mind, until I could no longer function. The people I knew, the places I lived, the jobs I had, the memories of the past that crept in slowly until one day it was like a storm, leaving behind the debris that was me crying until there were no more tears, feeling sad and hurt until there were no feelings left. I did not know how to care or how to love myself, or anyone else.

Here is the tricky part: whenever I experienced loss, my standard answer was "I'm okay," when really, I was not okay. It was a mask that I wore. I was in disguise, so no one knew how much I was hurting. It looked like I was cold and did not care for anything or anyone, which was the farthest thing from the truth.

Before I move on, let me ask you to reflect and think about what grief looks like for you. What exactly is it doing to how you function in life? I can surely talk at length to where it all leads and today, I am grateful I have lived through the storm and now the seas are calm and filled with beauty. Those ugly thoughts were like seeds planted in my mind, until I weeded my garden, leaving my mind filled with only positive memories. That is not to say that it was an easy journey. I didn't always know I had scars that needed healing to be able to move forward with acceptance, love and forgiveness.

Think about it, when you lose someone or something, it hurts, and it is dark and feels lonely. This is grief. To accept this too shall pass, one must confront what is really going on, because it does not melt away like an ice cube in the sun.

What did an emotional breakdown look like for me? I felt helpless and stuck, unable to move forward. Even today I can find lots of information on an emotional meltdown. However, attached to emotional breakdown is nervous (mental) breakdown. I remember not understanding that at all.

One day I was so stressed, I was about to end another relationship and my heart was pounding. I looked at my husband and said, "I'm going to have a heart attack." He answered, "I am not afraid of you having a heart attack. I am concerned that you will have a nervous breakdown! And, then it will be a very long and hard recovery." We spoke at length, but I remember what impacted me the most was my mind was in danger. You see what I valued and took pride in the most, my mind and its intelligence.

What happened over the next several years hurt. I feel grateful today to say it ended with a new awareness and fulfillment, but it did not start that way originally. It all began the day I could not function and my emotions finally got the best of me. I would scream and get so angry, reacting to things that did not even make sense to me. I was overwhelmed with anxiety and was very moody. I was warned to be careful, because I was, "on the verge of a nervous breakdown", or told that, "you are in a depression." So, with these warnings swirling in my head, off to the doctor I went.

I was sad and felt broken, as the doctor shared, "you are in a depression". I asked, "What is that and how long will this last?" The doctor did not answer, she continued and shared, "you are having a nervous breakdown." Again, I asked "What is that and how long will this last?" My thoughts were bombarding my brain but through the confusion I recall, "Oh no, I don't like this. What caused this?" Today, I know that it was grief stacked on top of grief, and no, it was not depression or a nervous breakdown it was a total emotional breakdown, or as sung by Bonnie Tyler, *A Total Eclipse of the Heart*, caused by an accumulation of unanswered, ignored, or overlooked grief.

Imagine all this hurt happened over a 60 year period. Out of it, I have learned so much. When asked the question "are you grieving"? I would answer, "maybe, I don't think so. My dad died but that was many years ago". Then came these words from the doctor, "Grief does not have a time frame." This was the journey of awareness and that was one of my earliest realizations. Now, here is the next part, at no time did the psychologist indicate that I was having an emotional breakdown, not then and not now. Also, when you speak to a professional, unlike grief, you do have a time limit, you are on the clock, so whatever happens in those minutes, stops until the next session. I was left with a lot of questions and fear. Thank God for books, for I read a lot and learned so much. I had to start looking at my whole life, but I caution you that it was the hardest thing I ever did. I don't know if I would suggest anyone do this on their own. This is just my story. I continued with that psychologist and did lots of reading for a year.

Back to my journey. How is this possible, I would ask myself. I can't be grieving for something that happened so long ago, can I? Grief now, that was a shock from when my dad died, over eight years prior. How could that be? It was a curious situation that was not logical to me.

I learned that grief was not only about physical death, but it was also about loss, loss of all kinds of stuff. A job, a sold house, a friend moving, relocating, a change. Although we may like where we are it does not discount what is no longer there. And that is a glimpse into grief. Also, grief is different for everybody. No two people experience it the same way and it is not something that can be explained easily in a book chapter or course module. If anyone tries to sell you a fast easy cure for grief, run!

All this gave me a lot to think about, no time limit, and how wide-ranging grief was. The impact that it had was hard to fully comprehend. All the reactions I experienced over the years left me exhausted. Not only that, but the reactions of others who I loved —they were also grieving because of what they saw happening to me, made me feel as though I was letting them down. At times, it seemed there was no end in sight.

From time to time, I would experience grief unknowingly. I did not label it as such. I would say, "I can't feel my heart anymore. It is like a tomato that someone squished and it hurts." Really, I was experiencing loss in some form, and it was easier to shut out and ignore the true feelings - really delaying the inevitable sadness that I had to go through.

I was wondering whether this feeling of sadness and loneliness could really be a result of grief, and what exactly did that look like. It was very surprising to learn grief was cumulative, that everything that happened to me had stacked up, and caused these feelings which left me mentally, physically and emotionally drained. All those losses, the friends that were transitioned through death, or the friends that were no longer in my life and still alive, the jobs I lost by choice or chosen for me, the family who left and no longer in my life, the opportunities and on and on the list went.

When I reflect on the people that were no longer in my life that were living, it was not understandable to me. They were hurt, I was hurt, and we could not get past the differences. We could not be in each other's company. which left me angry at first. Angry at them, and then blaming myself. The guilt it created was unbearable, until I realized that we had just moved on, and there was no one to blame. Grief all the same. Hurt and loneliness. The feeling that someone or something was gone, and I was helpless to change it.

As I write this today, I realize there is always a newfound awareness. When I was living these events and until now, I did not recognize the shock of it all, and that affects the body which also explains the fatigue. There was a feeling of being helpless and hopeless that also drained me and left me empty and lonely.

When I reflect on that time, another thought comes to mind. Not only did it all stack up, but when I experienced loss again, it was as if I was reliving all those negative emotions once again, not only for that one thing or person that I was losing, but the past experiences, once again. It was like a skip on an old record, leaving me with the same hurt again and again, and again. So that really does explain why it got worse and worse with each loss. An example of this was the emptiness and loneliness was overwhelming, and hit me when my mom was diagnosed with dementia. She was my best friend, and when it all started, I was in denial. I could not see it and did not want to see it. I searched for the moments to validate that she was fine, that she remembered me, or that her mind was not broken with dementia. I waited for each instant, in hope of a good day. With her I learned that the grief of finding out someone you love appears before, stays with you during, and lasts for a long time after the person is gone. I was grieving my mom while she was still living and could not show the fear I was filled with, for I needed her to be unafraid.

At one point, I reflected on my life and the losses and realized the very sad moments, in which I felt loss, was not only death. I knew I did not let go easily. That was another journey. I learned through divorce that the only way I could let go was with love. I could move forward only after going through the anger, and sadness, still love the person for what I had, and only then could I move on.

That's not the only thing I learned. It was realizing that it was not always the actual loss, but everything leading up to the loss which stacked up, and was the real cause of this emotional breakdown. Sometimes it's the fear or anticipation of the loss, the sleepless nights filled with anxiety, which were far worse than the event itself. During those times where I could only cry, sometimes for a very long time and then could not cry at all, were all adding to that stack of negative emotions that I was building. The shock that my body felt when I learned that I was losing someone was devastating, even before it happened.

If events leading up to a loss are not bad enough, sometimes it's the events following a loss that get you. The first Christmas, Mother's Day, or Father's Day, or Birthday after they leave. All moments to relive the pain if you're not ready.

The people I grieved for left me emotional and emotionless for far too long. Today, I realize it is not only about them not being here, but the feelings they instilled in me that I was missing. You see, whenever I had a loss, I thought I'd never feel my heart again. I was extremely strong outside but inside I was torn to pieces. I struggled with letting go.

Here are a few examples of the stories of what I lost as people transitioned from the human form:

These were the words I heard left me when my grandfather (my papa) died, "Stop the world, because Kim's here". He made me feel special, fantastic and I miss him. He gave me pure love, a great sense of security and confidence. I felt the loss not only of his physical presence, but his emotional and spiritual presence. With his death I thought, "who's going to take long walks with me, and not pick me up when I am tired, but make me and my legs strong?" He gave me resilience and today with all my faculties and senses I know that I am resilient. However, I doubted it at that time, thinking I did not only lose him, but all the strength in my legs as well. When I was afraid, he would say, "I'll go with you." I thought at the time that maybe there would not be another St. Patrick's Day celebration like we used to have. He used to tell me that I would be the Queen of the Irish Parade in Montreal one day. I surely was a Queen to him.

My granny, "Who was going to spoil me and love me unconditionally?" Fear crept in.

My uncle, "Who is going to protect me?"

My dad, "Who is going to think I'm perfect?"

My mom, "Who is going to be my friend?"

These examples show that the loss is more than the thing or person you obviously lost. It is all they represented as well. The impact on one's life because of the fear it leaves buried in our subconscious mind. For years after my grandfather died, I was scared to lose my granny and couldn't go into her house. I hated it there. I blamed my grandfather's death on the bad fall he had in the bathroom of that home. She also fell and broke her hip, and that was the beginning of the end of her life on this earth. So, now on top of grief I have guilt for the times I missed.

Letting go of another person, through death, a move or someone following another path, is hard. If forced upon you when you are not ready, it is even harder and can create bitterness. Help yourself, if someone is leaving then wish them well, even if you know where they are going won't be such a great place. There is bad out there, but my hope for my children is that they have some manageable obstacles to learn their lessons and that they have the wisdom to learn from others' mistakes. **May the opportunities be plenty.**

As I come to the end of this chapter, I'll share with you that throughout my life I could not even say goodbye when I left a room. There were no goodbyes, for they left me sad. I started to write a song many years ago at the pond in Massey Drive, Newfoundland. I continued the chorus on the road going from my husband's parent's house to his grandmothers in Random Island, Newfoundland. The lyrics give you a glimpse into my thoughts and feelings as they relate to love and goodbyes.

> *When I saw you there, I felt like I was home,*
> *And oh, right here I am not alone,*
> *When I look in your eyes I knew you before,*
> *There were no goodbyes to close love's door.*
> KATHERINE KIM MULLIN

You see, I don't like goodbyes. I can handle, "see you later" and this reflects no closing doors, and allows me to stay true to myself and to my beliefs. My friends know me, and only sometimes do they call me on it, especially when I hang up from a phone call too quickly.

Coincidentally, as I'm writing this, yesterday, my nephew who has been much like me his whole life, caused me to question my practice. You see, he would not say goodbye to me either. Then yesterday, as I was leaving, he hugged me and said, "I came back in. I know you don't like goodbyes, but I did not want to leave without a hug." So, it seems I have a lot to learn about healthy goodbyes and moving on without feeling sad.

I will leave you with what I believe is the secret weapon that helped me get to where I am now, which is emotionally healthy.

- I take care of myself and focus on what I want for my mind, body, soul, social, financial, adventures, and creativity. I stay true to what I want, with no apologies.

- I wrapped myself in a quilt that my husband made for me. 200 hours of work, and 1000 pieces of material, and a whole lot of love was poured into it, and it saved me.

- I have a statement that reminds me of what to do to stay emotionally healthy, so that I'm not draining my physical, mental, spiritual, or emotional batteries.

> *Accept the unacceptable,*
> *love the unlovable,*
> *forgive the unforgivable,*
> *and move on.*

Before I finish, I want to share that growth happens in the least expected places, and today I look back and can connect the dots and see that the person I am today with such abundance, love and happiness is a result of all I have experienced and one can see it as bad I choose to look at the positivity of it, I am continually seeking more and always satisfied with what is. My present moments are cherished and there are so many beautiful humans a phone call away at all times, we really are all united, what I want for me I want for you if it advances your growth.

I love my life and believe we live all things for a reason. Our path is the reason we become who we are. We can never be ready in advance when it comes to grief, we just need to face it and recognize when it plays its part on our journey.

Sending you light and love from my home to yours.

Katherine Kim Mullin

Katherine Kim Mullin is a philosopher, author, investor, perpetual student and lives life by design. She is passionate, loves life and people, and plays full out in everything she does. Katherine feeds her mind every day through reading with the intention to learn and grow.

Katherine is a businessperson with an entrepreneurial spirit with 35+ years in human resources and expertise in Commercial Real Estate Leasing. Her successful business colleagues and friends describe her as a prescient. Her success came from listening to her intuition and using her imagination while having the clarity to see the future. Another colleague and friend shared this with her "Katherine your head may be in the clouds, but remember your feet are firmly planted" which describes her well. Katherine Kim Mullin imagines a world in which everyone has wealth and connectivity.

Visit with Katherine Kim Mullin:

Website: www.katherinekimmullin.com

Facebook Group: https://www.facebook.com/ groups/1081112002499609

YouTube Channel: https://www.youtube.com/@katherinekim-mullin9588

A gift: She has a workbook that goes with her podcast which you can access with this link: https://www.katherinekimmullin.com/podcast

You can find her podcast Season 1: Are You Stuck on the You-Tube Channel

LIFE GOES ON, WITHOUT MY BROTHER

Linda Terjesen

On May 28th, 2006, after contacting the police in Orange County, New York I received a return call with words no one ever wants to hear.

When the call ended. I turned to my mom and said, "He's gone."

I remember it as if it were yesterday. My mom, her husband Ron, and I were in Laguna Beach.

Mom hadn't been able to get a hold of my brother Frank since the day before, and she was worried. She urged me to do something, and I started calling around to local hospitals in New York, and then finally to the police. It was Memorial Day weekend, and the police were busy. After sitting around in my apartment, I suggested we go to Laguna Beach to get outside and let our thoughts go elsewhere.

We'd only been there for about an hour when my phone rang. The police were calling me back. We were in a clothing store and the music was loud, so the police asked me to go somewhere quiet. I quickly walked into an art gallery next door, with Mom and Ron following.

The police went to my brother's house. The door was unlocked. They walked in and found Frank in his bed. No longer breathing. His dog was there in the house.

I remember my mom's reaction when the words "He's gone" came out of my mouth. She screamed "no" and threw her sunglasses on the floor. I picked up her sunglasses and Ron held my mom in his arms. She was hyperventilating and the woman who was working in the store came over and talked with us and gave my mom some water. The whole thing was so unreal. I was in shock.

Mom and Ron waited in the art gallery while I walked many blocks to get my car. I picked them up and drove through what felt like endless traffic back to my apartment.

I made all the calls. To my sister in Norway who would relay the news in person to our dad. To other family members, including my brother's oldest daughter. Then I booked flights for us to fly the following day from California to New York.

Frank passed away just two weeks after his 45th birthday. My dad had been there to celebrate with him as they shared the same birthday, May 10th.

No parent should ever have to lose their child. Having no children myself, I can't even begin to imagine the pain my parents went through for the rest of their lives.

My brother had a lot of stress in his life. It started years prior with his wife leaving him and taking two of their three kids with her to move in with her new police officer boyfriend, some guy she had dated in high school. One day Frank came home from work to an empty house. He didn't even know where his family was for days. My brother fought to see his two youngest children, who were brainwashed by their mother. She told a lot of lies so my brother struggled to get visitation rights and to maintain a close relationship with his children, who were clearly confused about what was going on and what the truth was.

Unhappy while living in Norway with the circumstances of a broken up family, one day my brother decided to leave and move to New York. After a few years living on Staten Island, he moved to a small town in Orange County, New York. Oddly enough, I lived in Orange County, California.

Frank had his own construction company, and the day he passed away he was working, laying tile in a house about ten minutes away from his home. When he didn't feel well, he told the woman he was working for that he had chest pains and that he'd go home and come back to her house later.

TIP: If anyone ever tells you they have chest pains, please call 911.

Frank's death likely could've been avoided.

Growing up, our family didn't talk much about feelings. We were raised to be independent and strong. We lived our daily life, went to school, and helped at home. We were raised to work hard, listen to, obey, and respect our parents.

Our dad raised Frank to be a tough guy, to never cry, which created both stress and a tendency to ignore pain when he shouldn't. Perhaps if he'd been raised differently, had listened to his feelings and asked for help, he'd still be here. What if, instead of driving home and going to bed, he'd driven straight to the hospital? What if the woman he was working for had called 911? We'll never know.

Life wasn't easy for my brother. He worked hard and long hours to provide for his family, and stayed in a marriage that obviously wasn't a happy one.

Frank did what he knew, what he was told, and what he thought was right. He knew heart disease runs in our family. He went to the doctor, he took his high blood pressure medications, and he monitored his blood pressure at home. He even had an EKG three days prior to passing away. None of it was enough.

I don't believe Frank's doctor was the best doctor for him and he could've done more to help my brother. When I requested Frank's health records, it took six months for them to be sent. I later learned the cutoff to file a lawsuit against my brother's doctor was six months. My thoughts about this doctor not being the best doctor were confirmed.

After Frank's death, I decided to get more serious about my own health. For years I'd been passionate about exercise, eating healthy, and overall health. I decided to take it further.

I was scheduled to start college in the fall of 2006, and my first class was a health class. From there I went on to obtain a Bachelor's Degree in Human Communications, followed by two Associate Degrees in Kinesiology and Nutrition, a Certificate of Nutrition, a Yoga Certificate, and I earned two awards in Coaching and in Athletic Training. I wanted to educate myself well before I incorporated my company, LTLTE, which stands for Learn to Love to Exercise.

When I started out, my goal was to help middle-aged men, like my brother, who suffered from heart disease and high blood pressure. That was a tough market to enter, so I ended up working with both middle-aged men and women, along with some younger women. After six years of coaching, I have found my niche working with women over 50 who want to improve their health and lose weight.

At 57 years old, having lost 20 pounds myself and maintaining my weight loss for over 24 years, the majority of my clients come to me for my expertise around sustainable weight loss. Our work goes much deeper than that, as weight loss has so much to do with long term behavioral change. I've developed a fat loss method that works, and I practice what I preach, setting a healthy example for my clients.

My brother is and always will be my purpose for helping others improve their health.

An area where I personally have had a lot of growth is awareness. It's also one of the most important areas where my clients expand. Together we work on strategies to achieve a client's goal and to make sure they are on the right path to success. Personal awareness reminds you to take responsibility for your own actions and feelings, and to persevere.

Where you place your attention is where you place your energy. It's about consistently making small, positive changes to develop new habits. When you realize there are consequences for your decisions and actions, you are likely more determined to work on making positive adjustments. With greater self-awareness it is easier to start thinking about implementing changes, as you realize you are the only one holding yourself back. Before you can change you have to recognize that there is a problem, be open to solving it, and be willing to put in the work to receive the results.

"He's gone." The words echo in my head.

My brother knew there was a problem, but wasn't aware of the severity of it all. The lack of awareness prevented Frank from being a stronger advocate of his own health.

When it comes to living your best life mentally, emotionally, physically, and spiritually it's up to everyone to take personal responsibility; granted there are sick and elderly people who cannot fend for themselves and need assistance. Some people are in great shape physically and yet they suffer mentally. Others are emotionally strong, with a regular spiritual practice, but physically they are not in good health. It takes consistent work to balance all four areas and to live a healthy life. With support and accountability it's much easier to stay on track.

There's always room for improvement, and it's never too late and you're never too old to get started. I can't think of a greater use of your time, effort and money than investing it in yourself. I am a big believer in personal development and continuous mindset work throughout life. My entrepreneurial journey has been my greatest teacher so far, and I work on myself daily to improve, and to have the capacity to have good energy and share it with everyone around me.

Physical fitness is something I practice and preach. One of the best decisions I've ever made was to join a gym, and for over thirty-three years I've gone consistently. It's easy for me to go to the gym on a regular basis as a workout always makes me feel better, stronger and more confident.

It can be easy to blame someone else for your illnesses, diseases, and shortcomings, but when you decide to take personal responsibility and think about what you can do to make your situation better, and ask for help, the journey will be more straightforward. Focus on what you have control over, such as your own attitude, responses, actions, and approach.

Some years after my brother passed away I went to a new doctor for a physical. As soon as she found out my family history, she insisted I have an EKG. Then she put me on medication for elevated blood pressure. I was determined not to stay on the medication. With monitoring my blood pressure at home and noticing it dropping too low, I decided to cut the pill in half. Simultaneously, I improved my diet and changed up my exercise strategy. My blood pressure kept dropping and my doctor agreed I could eliminate the medication.

I've already mentioned heart disease runs in my family. You may believe heart disease or high cholesterol running in your family means you're destined to have it as well. That is not my belief, and I have proof of the contrary.

It's important to take matters into your own hands. Doctors are paid and educated to prescribe medication, to treat the symptoms, but not the root cause. If we can work on solving the cause of a disease versus treating the symptoms with medications, we can save a lot of lives. Many doctors are not educated on, nor do they practice healthy eating or exercise. Doctors have a short allotment of time designated for each patient, and there isn't much time to get into details or discussions. Sadly, the easiest and most common solution is a prescription. Sometimes you may need a prescription, but I'm all about seeking natural alternatives whenever possible and most importantly working on solving the root cause.

Lifestyle choices can help you live a better life mentally, emotionally, physically, and spiritually. Proper nutrition and consistent exercise can reduce and eliminate hypertension and many other diseases and illnesses, reduce the need for medications, help reduce stress and improve sleep. Medications have a tremendous amount of side effects, and their band-aid solutions can sometimes cause more harm than good, leaving you with constipation, dizziness, headaches, drowsiness, muscle pain and more. Rarely do people read the medication pamphlets making them unaware of the lengthy list of side effects.

There's a lot of information you can access for free on the Internet. You can do an extensive amount of research to educate yourself, and find solutions; however some of what you come across may not be the most effective or efficient strategy for your goals, needs, and limitations. It's also easy to get confused and overwhelmed by all the conflicting information out there, and a confused and overwhelmed person typically does nothing and thus remains the same.

I became a coach so that I can provide my clients with a custom strategy, as well as educate them so they can understand the framework of their plan, and follow along well informed. My goal is to help my clients reduce and eliminate medications whenever possible. By changing their lifestyle and working from the inside out, the root cause of many diseases and illnesses can be cured, leading them to live a better, healthier, and longer life.

At my recommendation, one of my clients emailed her doctor asking to be taken off a statin, as she no longer has high cholesterol. This same client has auto-immune issues and her doctor hasn't tested her vitamin D levels, which helps regulate the immune system. It's important to be your own health advocate, because unless you're aware and you ask your doctor questions, you may be taking unnecessary medications for too long and living with their side effects.

My personal goal is to stay off medications for as long as humanly possible. I even helped my elderly mom reduce her cholesterol by changing her diet, even though her doctor insisted her issues were genetic, and unavoidable. To solve problems, we need to communicate, find solutions and take different actions.

After my dad passed away and I was at my sister's house I remember attempting to talk with my sister about my feelings about some differences she and I had, and she wasn't interested in talking about it. It seems much easier to just go along and live our daily lives, avoid talking about what's uncomfortable, and keep a lot of our feelings bottled up inside of us, where they may boil up until one day they erupt.

As I've grown older, and I'd like to think wiser, I've suffered many losses. I find talking about them helps. I think it's important to work through the grief, and when the tears come, I set them free. The other evening when I went for a walk I saw an elderly woman and her son together. I thought of my brother and my mother, and the tears came. I don't hold back my tears, and I think it's healthy to let out our emotions and talk about our feelings so we can better heal.

Talking about feelings is uncomfortable and many people don't like to be uncomfortable. Learning about yourself and personal growth is all about getting out of your comfort zone. With education, personal development, coaching, and entrepreneurship I've learned to communicate more effectively, which continues to be an important part of my growth.

My client journeys include communication, sharing, and celebrations. I love to hear my clients celebrate their victories with weight loss and health improvements. They don't always feel like they have something to celebrate, but as I give them a little nudge, they're reminded of more than one win. As they share it helps inspire the other clients in our community, leaving the client who shared feeling even more proud of their accomplishments.

I've found many women in their fifties aren't used to celebrating themselves, and that's an even bigger reason why it's important to start celebrating now. My goal is to help my clients feel amazing from the inside out, and the work starts in the mind. Excellent health is a mind-body connection as our emotions influence our health and longevity. Our thoughts, feelings, beliefs, and attitudes can positively or negatively affect our health and mental state. The actions we choose to take, such as eating healthy and exercising have a reciprocal impact on our mind and body.

It's your choice how you let your mind influence your body, and vice versa. Of course, it's easier said than done, but there are many effective therapies such as yoga, meditation, prayer, journaling, practicing gratitude, a relaxing walk in nature, and support groups that can help you feel better mentally, emotionally, physically, and spiritually. Exercise is one of the best methods to release stress and to increase energy. I take multiple short walks daily to manage my stress and to give myself a burst of energy.

"He's gone."

I remember when my brother lived in Norway, and he biked into town to go to a swimming hall. When he first lived in New York and had a lady friend, they ate a lot of vegetarian and pescetarian foods together. Those healthy actions helped his heart. When he was alone, I think he was struggling more emotionally, putting too much stress on his heart with working hard and long hours for clients and on his own house that he was fixing up. He rewarded himself with too much red meat, processed food and beer, which led to at least one episode of gout. Frank's last dinner was at a local bar in Monroe where he had a cheeseburger, fries, and a beer on a Friday after work, all of which challenged his heart condition.

Life is filled with what ifs, and for me, one of the biggest what ifs is, what if I'd known then what I know now? What if I could've helped my brother save his life with improved nutrition and regular exercise?

On a positive note, I've taken the devastation of losing my only brother and turned it into my passion to help others improve their lives.

Always remember you are unique, and you are the most important person there is. Ask yourself where you can improve your health and take greater responsibility. Start a new healthy habit for yourself, one that'll support you more mentally, emotionally, physically, or spiritually or a combination of all of those.

If you already have some good healthy habits in place, congratulations! I encourage you to challenge yourself to go a little further, do something different, introduce a new activity or healthy food into your life. You can help encourage and inspire others around you.

I dedicate this chapter to my loving brother Frank, such a kind hearted man, whose life was cut short. Yes, "He's gone," though in every part of the life I'm living for myself and my clients, "He's here."

Follow me here:

Instagram: @FitwithLinda

Facebook: Linda.Terjesen

Facebook group: LTLTE

Website: www.LTLTE.com

YouTube: www.YouTube.com/c/LTLTE

Linda Terjesen

Linda Terjesen is the Founder and CEO of LTLTE, Inc. (Learn to Love to Exercise), a company born out of her passion for health and fitness.

As a Certified Nutritionist, Weight Loss Expert, Online Health and Life Coach, and Certified Positive Psychology Coach for Women over 50, Linda empowers women worldwide to live their best lives, by improving their health working from the inside out.

Linda's journey began with her own struggles, once disliking exercise, then learning to love it over time. At age 57, Linda is in the best shape of her life, weighing 20 pounds less than she did at age 32.

Originally from Norway, Linda now calls sunny Southern California home.

Through LTLTE, Linda is on a mission to educate women on the importance of nutrition and exercise, showing that it's never too late and you're never too old to change your health and your life.

Linda's dedication stems from a deeply personal story of losing her only brother, Frank, to a sudden heart attack at age 45. LT-LTE is her tribute to him and her drive to help others avoid similar tragedies.

With a background in Human Communications and a string of health related degrees and certifications, Linda has the knowledge and heart to make the world a healthier place, one woman at a time.

I hope that Linda's story will inspire you, and as she says, "always remember, you are worthy of excellent health and by seeking help, you can reach your goals more effectively and efficiently."

SPEAK THE HEART

Marie Adell

*We gather life lessons like pearls on a necklace; each
shiny, round story forming a perfect opalescence
that showcases the beauty of our rich experiences.*

MARIE ADELL

YOU'RE A LIAR

Everything starts as a story because there's a story for everything.
It is a part of our origin, our birthright, our voice. A way to share
trials, tribulations, and triumphs of the human race. To pass along
wisdom and folly. Since the beginning of time, those before us told
stories to save lives, to be entertained. They told stories to take them
away from their own lives. We see stories played out in the televi-
sion, in the theater, on stages, and in our beloved books. They help
to transport us to places that we never could go otherwise. Take us
through time and space and everywhere in between. Storytelling
breathes life into our wildest fantasies and dreams, and sometimes
they come true. So why do we view storytelling by young children
as lying? Why do we shame, and feel so much shame around it?

She stood trembling in front of Him. Not a god, a man, though He
might have been as He was her judge, jury, and executioner. "Did
you do it?!" he demanded. A tiny 3-year-old shifted and shook
from the thunder of the voice and the knowledge of what was to
come. Standing there in her little nightgown, hair freshly wet from
the shower, wringing hands and wondering what to say that could
magically make this scene disappear. Make him not so angry, make
him not lose control and violate a body that did not belong to him.
Eyes darting, fingers fumbling, feet shifting back and forth. Dread
building in the pit of the stomach like a roaring fire. WHOOSH,
consuming the entire bitty being standing there without a defense.

Dearest reader, an experiment awaits you! From where you're sitting, stand up. Either enlist the help of a significant other or stand
in front of your refrigerator for something of larger stature. If

someone is assisting you, have them stand facing you. Stand facing your refrigerator otherwise. Bend down and support yourself on your knees and look up at the person or appliance before you. Notice where your body is in space and proximity to the person or metal. If it's a person, how close can you get, or have them get, before you feel your personal space being violated? Before it feels awkward and uncomfortable? Notice the height difference, either way. How far must you bend your neck upward, making the rest of your soft body vulnerable? How do muscles strain in your neck and chest? What vantage do you have? Now sit back on your heels. How does this change the view? The distance? The feel? Notice how your whole body feels. What sensations are going through you? Your chest, stomach, heart, head? If you are in front of the appliance, contemplate all of these things as well, noticing the sheer space this bulk takes up in front of you. Your inability to move out from under its shadow. The feel of its strength. Now stand up again. What emotions, feelings, sensations are you experiencing now?

The former is the view of a small child. Someone who cannot simply stand up and get out of an uncomfortable situation. Who is completely vulnerable in all places of their body simply by virtue of their view in their physical space. Who is completely dependent upon, and all at once at the whim, of this literal overlord.

"Did you do it?!" the voice shook her once more. Trembling she moved her head back and forth in a no; an attempt to make the situation disappear with the movement. Wrong answer. A large hand reached out like lightning and struck her in the side with force. "Don't lie!" The Voice thundered. "You'll only be punished more!" She wept desperately, lips quivering, body shaking. "Did you do it?!" once more rattled the air. Clearly He knew. There was no way around it. Head bowed, a slight nod, unable to even speak, so very choked up.

Lying is a NORMAL, natural part of child development. It is our discovery of being separate thinking beings from our caregivers. Lying is EXPERIMENTAL, helping us to gain understanding about morality, thinking of others, and how to make decisions. It also involves complex thinking, including: finding a way to gain attention, impress others, protect yourself from harm or pain, protect someone else from hurt or pain, or even help someone else to feel better about a situation. It helps us understand what we do and do not want in our lives.

Understanding and normalizing this developmental phase can create learning opportunities for both parent and child. So much shame is created around lying based on a religious philosophy, yet it is something everyone does in life! The next step is learning HOW to handle the conversation when "storytelling" (a much nicer, kinder, gentler way to explain what is really happening) is occurring, depending on the situation. This can be challenging for us as adults depending on how we grew up! Ask for help if this is the case. We don't have to know everything AND we can turn to resources to supplement our knowledge because we are caring, loving parents who want to support and nurture children and give them the gift of growing up loving themselves.

The memory of what happened next is blocked, locked away somewhere in the body as a secret, waiting to be released one day. A stain on the heart and in the brain. The Storyteller was beaten out of her. Burned at the stake to "save the soul." Thou shalt not lie was the reason. How many of us grow up the same? A reality desperately trying to be wished into existence? Sometimes from the absolute despair of terrible consequences. A third line right to experiment misunderstood in the land of Truth Seekers and Righteous Guards. Guards who did not uphold the same message for themselves. A voice snatched and silenced.

It is a marvel how our mind and body protect us from the truly terrible. The next scene, one of confusion. Tear stained shiny cheeks, sitting on a couch next to Him, feeling a mixture of relief, pain, and odd bonding. Eating popcorn and beginning to watch *The Ten Commandments* of yore, starring none other than Charlton Heston. Him calling me His buddy? Telling me He didn't want to do that to me? That it hurt Him more than it hurt me? Very, very, very confusing. As a child. Even as an adult looking back on the scene. Yet…

THE JOURNEY TO BE HEARD

When we know better, we do better. A straightforward, yet confusing mantra at the same time. Aren't we told things that we just don't do even if we know it will help us or others in our lives? It feels true yet we don't carry it out? Or someone shares advice and we choose not to take it? Don't we technically "know" it then?

It's what is going on with our children when we "tell" them something. Of course they cannot replicate it perfectly after the first time they are told. They do not have the experience nor the capability to carry out things with precision after just one chance. We need guidance, experimenting, repetition, practice, demonstration, and all kinds of other ways to imprint it within our bodies, our souls, to then be able to carry it out with ease; as a part of us. This goes for both things that will help us in life and things that we get "extra learning" experience from. EVEN when it involves the concept of storytelling.

We need to have permission to BE in our early years, so that we truly know how wonderful, awesome, great, and divine we are. "To err is to be human" (Alexander Pope). The rest of that phrase is "to forgive, divine." In order to be able to forgive others, we need to be able to forgive ourselves for being human first. When we are never given the opportunity to BE, to have a VOICE, it is difficult to give that to others. When we do not love our own being, our own voice, it is difficult to listen to others trying to find their own. And the reaction is to stifle, squash, control, punish.

Indeed, we do what we know. What has seeped down into our very DNA; the fabric of our physical existence. So even though we may have HEARD a better way, it doesn't mean it has worked its way down into the patchwork of our person. Let those without sin cast the first stone. Everybody commits acts that may be condemned by others. Yet when you truly love yourself and understand we are all one, we get to love even those who transgress against us because we can finally understand they ARE us. And they help to build us, shape us, mold us into what we have brought ourselves into this lifetime to do. Even to help us find our voice at the same time as it seems they are tearing it from our very throat.

The heart yearns to be heard, no matter how fervently another may try to silence it. No matter how we ourselves may try to silence it. Our stories will be heard. Demand to spill out. In our perspective; our perception. Even IF another determines it to be a lie.

A new baby is born. A mother determined to do things differently than the generations before. It doesn't come easily. It takes practice, patience, perseverance. It takes awareness, effort, and risk of alienation. It takes bravery. It takes finding her voice. A journey more perilous to the soul than any she'd taken thus far.

Growth is not for the faint of heart. Most of us go about our days bathing in the mundane and magnificent, yet remaining parched. Work is a distraction for the majority. Social media has become our main form of minute to minute entertainment. We thirst for more, never really quenched. Our mind becomes a cacophony of the noise surrounding us, our voices myna birds simply repeating what we hear in the form of gossip or as gospel.

We owe it to ourselves, and to our collective, to BE. Our nervous systems are begging us to tune in to ourselves and turn off the outside cacophony. How can we hear our own true voice if it is consistently being drowned in the energy of the masses? How can we access the vibrant vocalizations of our heart when we live in our headspace and allow others to live there rent free?

FINDING THE VOICE

Laughter floats over the playground and reaches the bench, sprinkling over in pixie dust particles of sweetness. The jungle gym full of squirming, climbing, limber little bodies in constant undulating motion. Shouts punctuating the still, baking summer air in staccato fashion with the rhythm of youth. Stamina is high and play ensues at length. As daylight begins to dwindle, her name is called out to catch attention and ready awareness for leaving. "Why is she calling you that name?" her newfound friend asks in confusion. "I don't know", she shrugs nonchalantly, staring intently, a slight imperceptible shake of her head accompanies a mild smirk across the face. A make believe name and identity being the cause of this bewilderment. Stretching her storytelling wings in comfort, confident they will not be clipped by her mother, who simply stands by in tickled amusement.

Words carry potent spells. Each one carefully crafted to signal to the Universe a chain reaction when combined together, yet powerful enough on their own to illuminate the former shadows. Names: words we label things, and people, and places. Identities we give to each item on this planet, in this realm, and beyond. Every word we speak on another gifts with kindness or pain, pleasure or shame, joy or guilt. In the end perception is everything. However the lens we embark on life with shapes our initial perspective, yet does not need to be the end result. Still, we get to be mindful.

"You are a liar," declared angrily by many. No seeking to understand. No empathy or sympathy. Mere black and white with no chance of color. A liar. This is who you are. Labeled and worn as a badge of shame for others to see and judge, surely, as if the invisible ink in which the words were painted were indeed a visible stain. Along with "thief," a "disappointment," an "embarrassment." Each word stung as a thousand yellow jackets must. Indignation, yet mixed with equal parts digestion. Half drinking the same belief flavor of kool aid. Unable to speak up on her own behalf, though her heart beat defiantly with the rhythm of unfair, unfair, unfair.

There is a frequency each word carries, and our vibration accepts or rejects that frequency, the tone absorbed or deflected based upon our place of understanding in space and time. Is this word meant for me or is it not? Do I identify with it or not? As children we are absorbing vocabulary, tone, mood and perspective at the speed of light. Fractals of phrases and meaning bouncing in and out of us as we discern and decipher this place we warped into. Too often we take the labels placed on us as children as our badge to carry, sewn onto our vest of life. What we do not understand until later, or maybe never, is that this is not our badge to carry. It belongs to the owner of the words. It is THEIR label for the way they feel about themselves.

Battered and bruised, broken bones, shattered soul; the boy longed for someone, anyone to stand up for him. "Bastard" instead of his given name. Treated like he did not, would not, ever belong. Trying to fit in, to please the unpleasable. A fight he was not armored for, a voice unheard, in a home unloved, with no protector. Storytelling stolen from him, too. Growing up, unable to shake the past from his hate-filled brain that was not there at the beginning of his life. Rage his outlet. His own children are the target. Trying to make them "better" so they would be "accepted" by others. Not understanding they only wanted to be accepted by him so they could love themselves. Unable to do so because the reflection they faced in his countenance showed them it was not possible in that place and time. He grows old, still self-loathing and lonely, convinced of his invisible battle of one for justice.

In order for our children to learn to love themselves and have a voice, they need to have role models showing them HOW. They need to see their worth, their value, their need to do nothing except BE themselves. How many rituals do we hold for ourselves and our families that mean absolutely nothing in the grand scheme of life, yet are scared to place our energy into ones that could mean true freedom for ourselves and our families in perpetuity? Which actually moves us further in the direction of the goals and dreams we desire for ourselves and them? That shows us the power we possess and has always been ours, and ultimately allows us to be a role model, an example, for our children too? Our divine right as creators.

Yet another call from the school. Another report of "misbehavior." That familiar uneasy feeling in the pit of the stomach, vestiges of yesteryear clinging to the gut, churning to the surface as a wreck brought back up in a storm. The adult, yet emotions stirring as though a child once again. That "in trouble" feeling, though it is not oneself this time; it's the next generation. How to soothe that feeling? What balm to use so that the moment can be felt presently? As the adult in the situation. So that the real child can be supported and less scathed by the circumstances. Utilizing tools gained. Recognizing and releasing the pain with gratitude. Breathing and becoming in tune. Ready to hold space and truly listen. So that HER voice can be heard. So that she does not know the sting of suppression, the shame of self.

SPEAK THE HEART

We cannot protect our children from everything. Even if we are creating generational transformation by being present, aware, thoughtful, mindful…all the things. Day after day they encounter the world. The world brings with it what the next generation has asked to mold and shape them into what they are meant to be. Yet.."it is not our job to toughen our children up to face a cruel and heartless world. It is our job to raise children who will make the world a little less cruel and heartless" as L.R. Knost so beautifully states. I'm not saying that the world is fully cruel and heartless - there are so many wonderful things out there. Yet creating a cushion, a soft place, where our children always know they can go and be fully accepted for everything they are.

We are all perfect, whole, and complete exactly as we are. Our voices are meant to be heard, and no matter the words coming forth, they are meant to create change in this world. Do we desire to be a catalyst for change in an uplifting way? Can we speak to ourselves more kindly and lovingly to echo that out into the world? Will we do this for ourselves? For the generations to come? How can we change our mindsets to reflect our beautiful souls?

Speak the heart.

Learn the language of the center of your being and free its voice.

> *So often times it happens that we live our lives in*
> *chains, and we never even know we have the key.*
> THE EAGLES

Sometimes we think we can do it on our own. Sometimes we realize we need the help of another resource or person.

We aren't meant to live in a bubble, and we don't. We get to do the hardest step and open our mouths and ask for help. Keep asking until we get what we need. Because once we do?

Let's see where your voice will take *you*.

Marie Adell

Marie Adell is a lifelong learner and practices using her voice to change not only her future, however also family futures. She is a teacher of early childhood, middle school, and special education for over 24 years, whose career has taken her around the globe. Two Master's degrees, an almost doctorate, and life lessons round out her education. International speaker, mother to a feisty and wise Manifestor daughter, wife, and now published author are labels to which she happily ascribes. You can find her on Facebook under Marie Adell, or on Instagram @growuwithmarie, although she is mostly word of mouth for her parenting program. Ask her how hundreds of families have utilized her methods to create generational transformation!

You can reach Marie on Facebook:
https://www.facebook.com/marieadellgrowu

Or Instagram: @growuwithmarie

Peace and vibrant energy

SEEKING THE HEART

LIVING HER BEST LIFE

An Interview with
Temple Grandin, Ph.D.

In an in-depth interview with Dr. Temple Grandin, she discussed highlights of personal adversity, overcoming challenges, and forging paths of triumph that illustrate "seeking the heart" in one's life.

Topic: Triumph through Visual Thinking, Autism Advocacy, and Embracing Different Minds

INTERVIEWER (I): *Dr. Grandin, thank you for joining me. Your book Visual Thinking underscores the significance of visual thought processes, especially for people on the autism spectrum. Today, I'd like to explore how these ideas unite in tales of triumph, both personal and societal.*

TEMPLE GRANDIN (TG): I'm delighted to speak about it. Triumph is a key word here because, in many ways, I had to discover how to succeed in a system not built for my visual style. Yet these differences propelled me to accomplish what I have.

I: *Before we discuss broader applications, let's start with your personal journey. You have often touched on early struggles—navigating autism at a time when there was minimal understanding. How did you triumph over that initial adversity?*

TG: For a long time, the word "autism" was like a closed door. I was told I might never speak, or that I wouldn't function "normally." My mother rejected those assumptions—she immersed me in structured activities, speech therapy, and also gave me hands-on experiences that matched my learning style. That set the stage for triumph. Even though it wasn't easy, the early exposure taught me discipline and confidence.

A pivotal triumph was when I recognized that my "pictures in the head" method, which once seemed odd to others, was actually a powerful asset for design and problem-solving. I overcame social and educational barriers precisely by leaning into that visual approach—what I later formalized in Visual Thinking. Sometimes adversity is the nudge that shows you your greatest strengths.

I: *You emphasize "leaning into" your visual perspective. How does that perspective guide you in moments of hardship or uncertainty?*

TG: When stress or doubt comes up, I go back to what I can visualize. For example, if I'm confronted with a complex livestock facility issue, I mentally run simulations in my head. If a challenge is social or emotional—like feeling overwhelmed by sensory input—I try to break it down into images that I can manage. Instead of drowning in abstract worry, I imagine each piece of the problem physically—like an item on a blueprint.

People sometimes forget we can "see" solutions. If you're a pattern thinker, you might approach adversity by analyzing repeating behaviors. If you're verbal, you might talk or write through it. My triumph lies in an ability to design or solve problems based on visually re-creating them in my mind. That's a technique I encourage others to discover—whatever their style might be.

I: *Seek The Heart is about finding personal victories. Could you share a story where your visual thinking directly led to a triumph in your professional work?*

TG: Certainly. Early in my career, I visited a slaughterhouse that had chronic issues with animals panicking. No one could pinpoint why the cattle were balking. Standing in the facility, I "became" the cow in my mind's eye—visualizing every angle from their point of view. I noticed they were spooked by a shiny reflection on a piece of metal, plus a chain that dangled overhead. It had never been considered relevant by the staff, but for the animals, it was terrifying.

Using that visual empathy, I convinced them to remove these distractions. The cattle instantly calmed. That was a direct triumph of visual thinking over a real industry problem. It validated that my "weird" way of seeing the world actually saved time, money, and reduced animal stress. That success fueled my confidence to keep going.

I: *It's a powerful example of how an outsider perspective—especially a visually oriented one—can transform an industry. Yet, you also mention exploring passions in an educational context. How can parents or teachers foster these "triumph stories" for children who might be struggling, whether they're autistic or simply different thinkers?*

TG: Schools often favor verbal and auditory teaching methods, leaving visual or kinesthetic learners in the dust. If you want to see children triumph, let them experience subjects in diverse ways:

1. **Hands-on Projects:** Building, drawing, or real-world problem-solving.

2. **Peer Collaboration:** A pattern thinker can pair with a strong verbal communicator to tackle a science project.

3. **Exploration of Individual Passions:** If a child loves trains, use that interest to teach math or geography.

Triumph arises when children discover they're good at something they enjoy. That fosters self-esteem, which in turn reduces the frustration or meltdown cycles we often see in kids who feel misunderstood. Seek The Heart taught me that "living your best life" is easier when educators appreciate and cultivate each child's mode of brilliance, instead of ignoring it.

I: *You mention meltdown cycles, which appear in Visual Thinking. Let's talk about personal adversity. Did you have meltdown moments, and how did you turn them into triumphant breakthroughs?*

TG: As a child, sensory overload could cause me meltdown after meltdown. Back then, I didn't have the emotional or verbal capacity to handle sudden changes or loud noises. My mother, mentors, and teachers incrementally taught me social rules and gave me a "safe" environment to decompress. That "safe environment" might be a small room with dimmer lights or an activity that deeply engaged me.

Turning meltdown into triumph also meant turning a tough situation into a learning moment. Instead of punishing me for meltdown behavior, supportive adults taught me coping strategies. Over time, I triumphed by seeing meltdown triggers as signals to reframe my environment or practice specific calming methods. If a meltdown can be seen as a signal—like a dashboard light—then you can address it systematically, just like I do with facility designs.

I: *What about caregivers or individuals who see no immediate way out of their chaos, medically or emotionally? You noted that "everyone has something unique." But how do they find hope if they're drowning in complexities?*

TG: The first step is acknowledging that someone out there shares that complexity, or at least some part of it. Communities—like autism support groups, specialized health forums, or professional circles—are essential. Getting stuck alone in your own fear hinders that triumph path.

Additionally, break large problems into smaller tasks. If you're overwhelmed, think visually: imagine each piece as a puzzle chunk. Each chunk can be delegated, or tackled in an ordered sequence. That method fosters a sense of progress. Also, track small wins. Even if the ultimate "fix" is months away, seeing incremental improvements boosts hope. There's a synergy between seeking the heart of what you love (the big "why" behind your fight) and the visual or methodical approach to daily steps.

I: *So your suggestion is: combine a "passion-based why" with strategic problem-solving that matches your thinking style. That leads me to ask: how do you personally define "living your best life," as you allude to in your writings?*

TG: For me, living my best life means maximizing the gifts I have to make real-world contributions. My contributions revolve around improving animal welfare, but that same principle can apply to anything. If you're verbally gifted, maybe your best life is about writing or public speaking that influences big changes. If you're tactile, you might create amazing crafts or solve mechanical issues.

It's also crucial to have a sense of autonomy—guiding your own path, even if it's unusual. Plus, I put a high value on constructive relationships with mentors, colleagues, and friends who respect me and give me space to excel as I am. That all fosters personal satisfaction, emotional stability, and a sense of purpose.

I: *Let's zoom out to the big picture: You've revolutionized the livestock industry, advocated for autism acceptance, and championed the recognition of diverse learning styles. That's a lot of triumph. If there's one takeaway from your perspective in Seek The Heart and Visual Thinking, what would you hope readers glean?*

TG: Takeaway: Our differences are not just "nice quirks." They're sources of innovation and empathy that can solve real, significant problems. When you or someone you love is labeled "different," that is often your key to forging a new path. So I want readers to see that each of us, in seeking the heart of who we are—whether we're an "object visualizer," a "pattern thinker," or a "verbal champion"—possesses the seeds of extraordinary triumph. We just need the right environment, mentors, and perseverance to make it bloom.

I: *That's beautifully said. Could you leave us with a personal anecdote that captures your sense of triumph in daily life—something small that might inspire everyday readers?*

TG: Sure. Not too long ago, I walked into a classroom of middle school students. One child, clearly anxious, asked me, "How can I be great if I don't fit in?" Right there, I sketched out a quick diagram of a curved chute. I said, "This chute existed in my head before anywhere else. I was an anxious child, too, but that anxiety transformed into the designs that help animals." The young student's face lit up.

That's triumph in miniature: when you see the spark of possibility ignite in another person's eyes because they realize their uniqueness is their advantage. Even small interactions like that can reshape how we all approach differences. For me, that's living the principle behind "visual thinking" and "seeking the heart" day by day.

I: *I love it! Dr. Temple Grandin, thank you for sharing these deeper insights and showing how your personal and professional triumphs are rooted in embracing your visual mind, while encouraging all of us to celebrate our distinct modes of thinking.*

TG: You're welcome. Remember, your mind is your superpower—use it well, and keep advocating for acceptance of all thinkers.

End of Interview

Dr. Temple Grandin

Temple Grandin is a Professor of Animal Science at Colorado State University. Facilities she has designed for handling livestock are used by many companies around the world. She has also been instrumental in implementing animal welfare auditing programs that are used by McDonalds, Wendy's, Whole Foods, and other corporations. Temple has appeared on numerous TV shows such as 20/20. Larry King Live, and Prime Time. Her books include: Thinking in Pictures, Livestock Handling and Transport *and* The Autistic Brain. *Her book* Animals in Translation *has been on the New York Times Bestseller List. Temple was inducted into the National Women's Hall of Fame in September 2017.*

CONCLUSION

Suzanne Sammon

When we speak about the heart, we remember that it is our cardiovascular system's main organ. The heart is responsible for a multitude of functions that keep our bodies supplied with essential nutrients and oxygen. The heart is a leader in our body and a networker. The heart is something we need to protect, cherish and value.

An amazing group of authors made the decision to collaborate on a book anthology regarding seeking the heart. Each author in this anthology had a specific heart mission. There were stories of resilience, courage, new journeys and inspirational lessons. The reader embarked on a path that arose from the heartfelt vulnerability within the content of these fearless chapters. Each author has given a piece of himself or herself that will continuously reverberate in the minds and hearts of those who dive into this extraordinary book.

From the very beginning, the reader was guided into an exploration of the inner treks of a group of individuals who had diverse life experiences and the desire to write about them. The reader was presented with paths where he or she was able to gain insight into a myriad of topics including physical health and wellness, executive functioning, grief, loss, and mental health conditions. And while the stories were distinct, they shared one pivotal commonality: each author spoke from the deepest part of the heart and soul.

Why do authors choose to contribute to a compilation?

Why does a group of writers from all over the world decide one day to go on a path like this?

The answers are:

- To lead.
- To provide a route to the reader's destination.

- To show people the way.

A book has the exceptional ability to create a global legacy; to reach billions of people within the mammoth scope of the technology available.

Books have staying power.

Books have carried on through history and affect the many lives who take the literary sojourn.

Books embrace readers into the lives of those whom they never would have encountered otherwise.

Hearts are changed for both the author and the reader.

What is the next step?

Seek the Heart wasn't simply a title. Rather, it was a calling. Each chapter pursued and spoke to the reader in whatever way it was meant to, which is the beauty and attractiveness of the written word.

Each author had a story to give.

Someone was impacted by that special story.

It was meant to be.

It was the hope and desire of each *Seek the Heart* author that the reader didn't just focus on the destinations of his or her journey, but instead embodied the essence of each life experience. There was much to be gained from this book when taken in the spirit of why it was originally put together. Every reader was meant to be inspired physically, emotionally and spiritually. There wasn't one chapter that was unrelatable. There wasn't one chapter where someone couldn't have it happen to them. These were compelling accounts that were meant to inspire and encourage.

Books change hearts.

Books save lives.

May the hearts of the authors and readers be forever valued and held in much strength always.

Suzanne Sammon
AUTHOR AND ENTREPRENEUR

Suzanne Sammon

Suzanne LaVoie Sammon is filled with a huge zest for life. She has served in multiple diverse industries, but her passions are for hospitality, tourism and customer service. Suzanne began her author journey in 2016 with solo and compilation books. Additional literary achievements include being a guest blogger for multiple digital magazines and websites. Suzanne serves in both traditional and freelance sectors, including serving as an international editor, proofreader and ghostwriter. She has been a public speaker at various venues (both in-person and online) and holds an advanced degree in international and community development. Suzanne has a love for helping customers/guests have epic experiences, especially through communication, promotion and attention to individual needs and preferences. Suzanne's level of expertise derives from a professional journey of over 30 years of customer service-related positions. Suzanne believes everyone can be their own individual tour guides, which enables them to navigate their own unique journeys toward epic destinations.

www.highrisetourism.com

www.digitalinnovatorsuzannesells.com

https://m.facebook.com/coolwritersuzanne/

https://www.instagram.com/tourismgurusuzannelavoie/

https://www.tiktok.com/@tourismgurusuzy

https://youtube.com/@digitalsuzie

RESOURCES

https://www.griefshare.org/

A GriefShare support group is a safe, welcoming place where people understand the difficult emotions of grief. Through this 13-week group, you'll discover what to expect in the days ahead and what's "normal" in grief. Since there are no neat, orderly stages of grief, you'll learn helpful ways of coping with grief, in all its unpredictability—and gain solid support each step of the way.

https://988lifeline.org

At the 988 Suicide & Crisis Lifeline, we understand that life's challenges can sometimes be difficult. Whether you're facing mental health struggles, emotional distress, alcohol or drug use concerns, or just need someone to talk to, our caring counselors are here for you. You are not alone.

disasterdistress.samhsa.gov

The national Disaster Distress Helpline is available for anyone experiencing emotional #distress related to natural or human-caused disasters. Call or text 1-800-985-5990 to be connected to a trained, caring counselor, 24/7/365.

https://www.crisistextline.org

Text HOME to 741741 and you'll be connected to a trained Crisis Counselor. Crisis Text Line provides free, text-based support 24/7.

https://www.thetrevorproject.org/

Call 1-866-488-7386 or text START to 678678. A national 24-hour, toll free confidential suicide hotline for LGBTQ youth.

https://www.211.org/about-us/your-local-211

If you need assistance finding food, paying for housing bills, accessing free childcare, or other essential services, visit 211.org or dial 211 to speak to someone who can help. Run by the United Way.

https://www.thehotline.org/resources/

For any victims and survivors who need support, call 1-800-799-7233 or 1-800-799-7233 for TTY, or if you're unable to speak safely, you can log onto thehotline.org or text LOVEIS to 22522.

https://rainn.org/about-national-sexual-assault-tele-phone-hotline

Call 800.656.HOPE (4673) to be connected with a trained staff member from a sexual assault service provider in your area.

https://www.caregiveraction.org/

Contact Caregiver Action Network's Care Support Team by dialing 855-227-3640. Staffed by caregiving experts, the Help Desk helps you find the right information you need to help you navigate your complex caregiving challenges. Caregiving experts are available 8:00 AM – 7:00 PM ET.

https://drugfree.org/

Call 1-855-378-4373 if you are having difficulty accessing support for your family, or a loved one struggling with addiction faces care or treatment challenges resulting from COVID-19 circumstances, the Partnership for Drug-free Kids' specialists can guide you. Support is available in English and Spanish, from 9:00 am -midnight ET week-days and noon-5:00 pm ET on weekends.

https://strongheartshelpline.org/get-help

Call 1-844-762-8483. The StrongHearts Native Helpline is a confidential and anonymous culturally-appropriate domestic violence and dating violence helpline for Native Americans, available every day from 7 a.m. to 10 p.m. CT.

https://celebraterecovery.com/

Celebrate Recovery is a safe place to find freedom from your hurts, hang-ups, and habits. Meet with a CR Group online from anywhere, every Wednesday at 12pm PST.

Our online Zoom group makes it possible for anyone to find the help they need, especially if there isn't a CR Group close to where you live, or if you need immediate encouragement in your recovery journey.

https://www.aa.org/

Have a problem with alcohol? There is a solution. A.A. has a simple program that works. It's based on one alcoholic helping another.

https://al-anon.org/

Al-Anon members are people, just like you, who are worried about someone with a drinking problem. Family members have the opportunity to learn from the experiences of others who have faced similar problems. Alateen Meetings: Teens come together to share experiences to find effective ways to cope with problems.

https://oa.org/

Overeaters Anonymous (OA) is a community of people who support each other in order to recover from compulsive eating and food behaviors. We welcome everyone who feels they have a problem with food.

ACKNOWLEDGMENTS

Kara O'Daniel

First and foremost I would like to thank my family. My partner Jon, my parents, and two siblings are my biggest supporters and I would not have even dreamt about doing a project like this without their incredible support. To my best friend Suzanne, who empowers and encourages me every single day to go after my dreams and reminds me that I am good enough to do amazing things in the world. Without her encouragement I probably wouldn't have started this project.

I want to thank all my therapists, especially my current one who helped me realize that compiling a book like this has been on my heart for a very long time and with their help I was able to take the necessary steps to take this dream out of my head and put it into action.

For years, I have wanted to create a safe space for people to share their stories of living their best life mentally, emotionally, physically and spiritually. *Seek the Heart* is exactly that! Some people have chosen to share their stories of overcoming obstacles, some, resources to improve your day to day life, and others share stories of what happened to their loved ones that changed their lives forever, but they all have one thing in common, they are all living their best life. I want to thank each and every author who poured their heart and soul into their chapter. The time and effort they put into their stories makes this book so special. The authors who contributed:

- Dr. Fern Kazlow
- Courtney Kaplan

- Christopher Birstler
- Destiny Shackleton
- K. Crystal Griffith
- Haley Gray
- David Vine
- Kelly Fritz
- David Hollingsworth
- Elaine Williams
- Karen Robinson
- Donna Palamar
- Francine Juhlin
- Heidi Livengood
- Katherine Kim Mullin
- Linda Terjesen
- Marie Adell
- Dr. Temple Grandin
- Suzanne Sammon

I also want to extend a thank you to our incredible editing team. Haley Gray, K. Crystal Griffith, and Dr. Fern Kazlow stepped up in a big way and were extremely helpful in getting this project to come to life! I would also like to extend a thank you to Rich Hopkins. Without him, this project would not have left the ground.

And to you, the reader. Thank you for taking the time to read each story and to allow yourself to feel all the feels that come with each chapter. Be transformed and inspired by each word and I hope you take away from reading this book that no matter the yuck that you go through in life, you will always come out the other side of it stronger!